De Vere is Shakespea

DENNIS BARON

Eight decades ago Edward de Vere, 17th Earl of Oxford, was identified as having written the works attributed to William Shakespeare. Further biographical evidence accumulated in Charlton Ogburn Jr.'s *The Mysterious William Shakespeare* (1984) provided more extensive documentary support. But evidence from the life of de Vere appeared to be insufficient proof to convince the Stratfordian establishment.

So Dennis Baron began to explore the poems and plays themselves for clues, with comparative evidence from other writers of the period. He wondered whether the writer's identification, suspected from his background, might be confirmed by the use of puns and wordplay from languages known to de Vere, in particular Latin, Italian and French.

Piece by piece the jigsaw of new evidence from the wordplay became complete, as over a thousand pages of incontrovertible proofs have been consolidated, then refined and presented concisely for the lay reader's benefit. The authorship debate intensifies.

Vested interests will ignore any amount of evidence, reaffirming that a barely literate grain merchant from Stratford wrote plays set at Court (where he may never have set foot), on the Continent of Europe (where he never travelled) and describing family circumstances and wealth enjoyed, and poverty endured, by the 17th Earl of Oxford.

However, the wordplay now discovered in great quantities far beyond the coincidental now makes it highly probable that de Vere is Shakespeare the writer. Dennis Baron's detailed step-by-step detection feats will fascinate all lovers of the Elizabethan period and Shakespeare. Understanding of the plays and poems will now become immeasurably enhanced by an appreciation of their content, true wit, depth and complexity.

✳

De Vere is Shakespeare

Evidence from the Biography and Wordplay

TRULY NOTHING TRUER

by DENNIS BARON

Introduced by Christopher H. Dams
The De Vere Society

THE OLEANDER PRESS
CAMBRIDGE ✳ NEW YORK

The Oleander Press
17 Stansgate Avenue
Cambridge CB2 2QZ
England

The Oleander Press
80 Eighth Avenue, Suite 303
New York
N.Y. 10011
U.S.A.

British Library Cataloguing in Publication Data

Baron, Dennis E.
De Vere is Shakespeare: evidence from the biography and
wordplay. – (Oleander language and literature series ; v. 19)
1. Shakespeare, William, 1564–1616 – Authorship – Oxford
theory   2. Oxford, Edward de Vere, Earl of   3. English
drama – Early modern and Elizabethan, 1500–1600
I. Title
822.3'3

ISBN 0-906672-37-6

Printed in Great Britain

Contents

Elizabeth I. Portrait by Marcus Gheeraerts the Younger. By courtesy of the National Portrait Gallery, London.

List of Illustrations

William Cecil, 1st Baron Burghley. Portrait by Marcus Gheeraerts the Younger. By courtesy of the National Portrait Gallery, London

Introduction
by
Christopher H. Dams

The entire written works of the greatest author in our language to have come down to us are six ill-written signatures, all different and indifferently formed. One of them is shown below:

There are no surviving letters from him and only one to him, which was not apparently sent; there are no records of anyone meeting him in a social context; there are no records of his having been paid for any play. These facts, you would think, might give us cause to consider whether the fame heaped upon William Shakspere of Stratford, as the playwright, is perhaps misplaced.

The case for attributing the plays and poems to Edward de Vere, 17th Earl of Oxford, writing under a pseudonym, rather than to Shakspere of Stratford, was made by a teacher of English in the Isle of Man, Thomas Looney, in 1920. His thesis was that authors are inevitably revealed in their works; that their personal experiences, characteristics and views of their world, when we know them, can be found reflected in their works, and that, conversely, it is reasonable to deduce them from the works if we do not know much about the author from other sources. This correspondence between life and works is a common enough observation, but when he put Shakespeare's works to the test, he found no such correspondence. His observation has always frustrated Shakespearean biographers.

To solve this conundrum, he first compiled a list of characteristics of Shakespeare which he deduced from the works. These were that he was a mature man of recognized genius, eccentric and rather mysterious, unconventional and of intense sensibility, but not much appreciated by his contemporaries – a man apart; on the other hand, a man of well-known literary tastes and enthusiasm for the theatre, and recognized by contemporaries as a lyric poet; a highly-educated person, particularly versed in the classics. He also detected that he must have been of the higher aristocracy, exhibiting a strong affinity with his feudal ancestry, especially the Lancastrian dynasty, and with probable sympathies for Catholicism, in a Protestant society; an enthusiast for Italy and things Italian; a sportsman, especially knowledgeable of aristocratic sports, and a music-lover; not a good manager of money, and one who experienced difficult relations with women.

When he tested these characteristics against what he knew for certain about William Shakspere of Stratford, as opposed to the myths and speculative stories which had built up around him, he found only one – connections with the theatre — reflected there, and concluded that this man could not have been the author. He searched the *Dictionary of National Biography* for another figure, flourishing in the second half of the 16th century, who did match his list of characteristics, and found Edward de Vere, who corresponded with all of them, and concluded, on the basis of that test only, that he had found the true author. Since Thomas Looney published his findings in

1920, they have never been refuted by Shakespearean scholars, and indeed further research has reinforced them. For example, de Vere's early poems were published, some without his consent, signed with his own title *The Earle of Oxford or Oxenforde* or variations on it such as *E.O., E. (of) Ox.* and *Vere.* These publications ceased in 1592, the year of publication of *Venus & Adonis* by William Shakespeare. Why?

This new book presents a unique contribution to those researches. In it Dennis Baron identifies, with many examples, a sub-text of multi-lingual puns, most of them in Latin, but some also in French, Italian and Spanish, on Edward de Vere's family name – which was spelt Vere or Ver – and his family motto *Vero Nihil Verius* or Nothing Truer than Truth, itself a multi-lingual pun on the name. This sub-text, he contends, runs through all the plays and poems of Shakespeare. The complexity and sophistication of these puns, he concludes, would have been beyond the intellectual capabilities, as they appear in the historical record, of Shakspere of Stratford. Indeed, they would have been pointless as references to him, so that their discovery reinforces the case for Edward de Vere as the playwright and poet.

He makes a further very important point. It is known that many of the plays were written for, and first performed at, Court. The courtly audience were all highly-educated people, particularly in the classics, able to read and write Latin fluently. Many of them, including the Queen and Edward de Vere, were able to hold conversations in Latin, and modern European languages. The existence and significance of the sub-text of puns, in plays written for their entertainment, would have been very clear to them, and would confirm what may have been an open secret, that Shakespeare was Edward de Vere's pseudonym. This sub-text would not be apparent to the groundlings, any more than it has been to modern audiences or readers, until now, and thus the pseudonym went undetected.

I believe that it was important to the Elizabethan

Establishment, for both social and political reasons, that the fact of Edward de Vere's authorship should not become public knowledge, but remain an open secret within the magic circle. This is not to argue a conspiracy theory: there was no need for a conspiracy. Elizabethan England was a police state, using torture and censorship of printing as two of its weapons to maintain control, reinforced by a kind of self-imposed censorship exercised by writers and printers. To those who object that such a secret could not have been kept without an elaborate conspiracy, I have only to recall the press silence on Edward VIII's relationship with Mrs Simpson during 1936; a silence preserved until the last moment, despite widespread reporting in America and on the Continent, and this without benefit of a police state, censorship or conspiracy. A more recent example is the silence, broken only recently, surrounding President John Kennedy's womanizing, which was an open secret in Washington at the time, although unknown outside the capital.

Mr Baron's book makes a major new contribution to our understanding and enjoyment of Shakespeare's works and of the world in which Edward de Vere wrote them, and I commend it to you.

✳   ✳   ✳

I WILL SHAKE-SPEARE
(crest of de Vere as Viscount Bulbeck)

I

The Life of Edward de Vere

I have written this book so that I can explain how Edward
de Vere, the seventeenth Earl of Oxford, identifies himself
as being William Shakespeare.

I have not written this book because I am trying to
prove that Edward de Vere was William Shakespeare. I do
not have to prove that the Earl of Oxford wrote the plays
attributed to Shakespeare, because the Earl of Oxford
proves it for himself, in his own words, the words of his
pseudonym, William Shakespeare.

In *As You Like It* (III.iii.11), Touchstone says: "When a
man's verses cannot be understood, or a man's good wit
seconded with the forward child, understanding, it strikes
a man more dead than a great reckoning in a little room".

The reference to "a great reckoning in a little room" is
a reference to the death of Christopher Marlowe; and the
meaning of the passage is that unless one has a pre-
knowledge of the wit that is in the work, then the writer
of the work will not only die, like Marlowe, but will be forgotten.

For almost four hundred years, the "wit" that is hidden in all of the works of Shakespeare has been lost, and
consequently, the man who was Shakespeare has been

forgotten. I have found this "wit" to be hidden in all of the works of Shakespeare and consequently, I have found the man who was Shakespeare.

Having found the hidden wit, I can say without a shadow of a doubt that the Earl of Oxford intended future generations to know that he was "Shakespeare"; and that "Shakespeare" was even more of a genius than even his most ardent admirers realize.

I could explain the wit in a few lines but, if I were to do so, some people might assume that it is far more difficult for them to understand than it actually is; and therefore, as I feel that everyone should understand the wit, I think it better to explain how I slowly stumbled upon this discovery over a period of several months.

Until a few years ago, like the majority of the population, I had always believed that Shakespeare, the writer of the plays, was the man who had been born in Stratford-upon-Avon in 1564. I believed this because it was what I had always been told. It never occurred to me to question why so few facts are known about the man, or his life.

My knowledge of the plays was fairly average. I had read only three or four of the plays at school, but I had read almost half of them in my late teens and early twenties. I had seen only about half a dozen live productions in the theatre, but I always watched television productions whenever possible.

Although I was no academic, I did feel that Shakespeare had a certain fascination: the fascination of trying to understand what it all actually means.

I had read, or heard, that some people believe that Shakespeare was Francis Bacon, and that another group of people believe that Shakespeare was Christopher Marlowe, but until a few years ago I had never even heard of Edward de Vere, the seventeenth Earl of Oxford, until late one night when I saw a television documentary programme about the controversy in the academic world concerning the authorship of the works of Shakespeare. One of the participants in the programme was the American writer Charlton Ogburn Jr., who had written a book in 1984 called *The Mysterious William Shakespeare* in which he had proposed that the Earl of Oxford was Shakespeare. Also on the programme was a well known Shakespearean academic who was presenting the established point of view; but I remember thinking that his arguments seemed to be very weak compared to those of Ogburn. I was so impressed with Ogburn's theory, and with his performance on the television programme, that I bought his book a few days later when I saw it on a shelf in my local bookshop.

Charlton Ogburn's book is in two sections. The first section deals with why William Shakespeare, the man born in Stratford-upon-Avon, could not have been William Shakespeare, the writer of the plays. The second section of Ogburn's book deals with why the Earl of Oxford is the most likely person to have been William Shakespeare. (Throughout this book I shall use the spelling Shakspere when referring to the man born in Stratford, and the spelling Shakespeare to denote the supposed author of the plays).

Ogburn says that the evidence that William Shakspere was not Shakespeare is better than the evidence that the Earl of Oxford was Shakespeare, although in my opinion he puts forward a very convincing argument in favour of the Earl of Oxford's having been Shakespeare.

The idea that Oxford could have been Shakespeare was first presented in 1920 by J. Thomas Looney, and over the years the main arguments in its favour have been that, because of his education and social position, and because many of the plots and sub-plots in the plays seem to be based on incidents in his life, he is the most likely person to have been Shakespeare.

Edward de Vere was born at Hedingham Castle, Essex, on 22 April 1550, the son of John, sixteenth Earl of Oxford, and Margaret Golding.

His father, as Lord Great Chamberlain, officiated at the coronation of Queen Mary in 1553, but he subsequently withdrew to the country for his own safety. He came out of retirement to escort Elizabeth from Hatfield to London, and officiated at her coronation in 1559. Elizabeth visited Hedingham Castle for five days in 1561, so that from an early age Edward de Vere was acquainted not only with Elizabeth and her royal court, but also with the politics of monarchy. The sixteenth Earl of Oxford died on 3 August 1562, leaving the Earldom and an impoverished estate to the twelve-year-old Edward de Vere.

However, the Earl of Leicester was granted all of the lands and estates of John de Vere, not permanently of course, but it was to be 26 years before he handed over to Edward de Vere the last of these lands and estates. The Earl of Oxford was made a royal ward in the care of Sir William Cecil, later Lord Burghley, Elizabeth's Principal Secretary of State, and he lived at Cecil House for the next eight and a half years, until the age of twenty-one. His mother married Charles Tyrrell within a few months of his father's death.

These events in the life of Edward de Vere were arranged and supervised by Elizabeth I, and it is these events, and the people involved in them, that provided the initial source and inspiration for *Hamlet*. Gertrude is a combination of Elizabeth I and Edward de Vere's mother. Claudius is a combination of the Earl of Leicester and Charles Tyrrell, who had the same surname as the man who murdered the princes in the tower, and it has long been accepted that Polonius is a caricature of Lord Burghley. This is why actors who play Polonius are traditionally dressed and made up to look like the portraits of Lord Burghley.

A record of de Vere's daily routine at Cecil House has been preserved in a document entitled *Orders for the Earl of Oxford's Exercises*, included in which were two hours each day for both Latin and French, as well as dancing, writing and drawing, cosmography, and exercises with his pen. At the age of fourteen he received his degree from St. John's College, Cambridge, and at sixteen an honorary Master of Arts degree from Oxford University. A year later he was admitted to Gray's Inn to study law.

In 1567 Edward de Vere's uncle, Arthur Golding, had published his translation of Ovid's *Metamorphoses*. All Shakespearean commentators agree that Ovid was the main influence on Shakespeare's style of writing, and therefore Arthur Golding's translation is today known as Shakespeare's Ovid, as it became the standard translation during Shakespeare's lifetime and must have been read by Shakespeare. Golding did not write anything else remotely like his translation of Ovid's *Metamorphoses*, which has been described as "somewhat curious English"; and therefore, it may have been written by his nephew, Edward de Vere.

In 1569 Thomas Underdowne dedicated to the Earl of Oxford his translation of *An Aethiopian Historie* by Heliodorus, dedicated not only for his known interest in history and learning, as Underdowne wrote, but also, presumably, because the Earl would have appreciated the translation from Greek to English.

The northern rebellion of 1569 was a plot by the northern Earls of Northumberland and Westmorland to march south and unite with the Duke of Alva, who would have crossed the channel from the Low Countries. Elizabeth was to have been deposed and replaced by Mary, Queen of Scots, who was to have married the Duke of Norfolk, a first cousin of the Earl of Oxford. However, in October, the Duke of Norfolk was imprisoned in the Tower by Elizabeth to await trial for treason. The rebellion went ahead as planned, but was eventually defeated in the spring of 1570.

Oxford wrote to William Cecil in November 1569 asking if he could serve "my Prince and country, as, at this present troublous time, a number are", but it was to be the end of March 1570 before he was allowed to see military action, probably with the Earl of Sussex at the siege of Hume Castle.

By 1571 Oxford had become one of the favourites of the Queen, excelling not only in languages, learning, literature, and the arts, but also at the tilt, tourney, and barriers. At a tournament before the Queen at Westminster, in which the challengers were the Earl of Oxford, Charles Howard, Sir Henry Lee, the Queen's champion, and Christopher Hatton, the chief honour was given to the Earl of Oxford. He was also reputed to be the finest dancer in the country, a skill particularly pleasing to Elizabeth who showed a lifelong interest in formal dancing.

After failing to arrange a marriage between his daughter Anne and Philip Sidney, the financial details of which seem to appear in the opening scenes of *The Merry Wives of Windsor*, William Cecil, with the help of Elizabeth I, seems to have arranged the marriage between Anne and the Earl of Oxford, as it was beneficial not only to the Earl of Oxford and Anne Cecil, but also to William Cecil. The Earl of Oxford was marrying into one of the new wealthy families of England, which for him, being in a state of relative poverty, must have been the main attraction of the marriage; and Anne Cecil was marrying into one of the foremost aristocratic families in the land. However, there was an obstacle to the marriage: one of the premier Earls of England could not marry the daughter of a commoner. This obstacle was easily overcome; four months before the proposed marriage, William Cecil was created Baron Burghley. This particular obstacle to the marriage is referred to in several of the plays of Shakespeare.

The marriage should have been in September 1571, but it was postponed, allegedly because the Earl of Oxford had planned the escape from the Tower of his cousin the Duke of Norfolk. The marriage did take place in December 1571, when Oxford was twenty-one, and Anne was fifteen. So, in actual life, Hamlet had married Ophelia the daughter of Polonius; but when he came to write the play some fifteen or twenty years later Oxford knew that the marriage had been a disaster, and so in the play Hamlet refuses to marry Ophelia.

Less than a month after the marriage the Earl of Oxford's cousin, the Duke of Norfolk, was brought to trial in Westminster Hall, charged with treason. Lord

Burghley, who had taken the leading role in bringing the Duke of Norfolk to trial, and remained active during the trial, demanded that Norfolk's life should be forfeited. The verdict of "guilty" was never in any doubt, and the sentence was death. The Earl of Oxford believed that his cousin should have been pardoned, and he blamed Burghley for having Norfolk executed.

Oxford's support for the Duke of Norfolk during the two years while Norfolk remained in the Tower waiting for his trial was one of the reasons why Oxford's marriage to Anne Cecil had been arranged by Burghley and Elizabeth: to neutralize Oxford's Catholic leanings within a Protestant family that was securely tied to the crown.

During the four weeks between his marriage and the trial of his cousin, the Duke of Norfolk, a book appeared which marked a significant step forward for the Earl of Oxford. This book was Bartholomew Clerke's translation from Italian to Latin of *Il Cortegiano* (The Courtier), by Castiglione. The Latin preface was written by Oxford, and headed with the full grandeur of his titles: "Edward Vere, Earl of Oxford, Lord Great Chamberlain of England, Viscount Bulbeck, and Baron Scales and Badlesmere, to the reader – Greeting".

Never before had an English Earl had his writings published under his own name during his own lifetime and, by presenting the preface under the full grandeur of his titles, he not only broke with tradition, but also announced to the world that he was a writer.

The following year Oxford wrote a preface to, and paid for the publication of, Thomas Bedingfield's translation from the Latin of the book he called *Cardanus Comfort*. This book has been called by an orthodox Shakespearean scholar, the late Hardin Craig, "Hamlet's book" because of the similarities between it and certain passages in *Hamlet*, particularly between Hamlet's famous soliloquy and this passage from *Cardanus Comfort*: "What should we account of death to be resembled to anything better than sleep . . . . Most assured it is that such sleep be most sweet as be most sound, for those are best wherein like unto dead men we dream nothing. The broken sleeps, the slumber, the dreams . . . . We are assured not only to sleep but also to die . . . . Only honesty and virtue of mind doth make a man happy, and only a cowardly and corrupt conscience do cause thine unhappiness".

Christopher Hatton had been one of the Queen's favourites, having come to court, they said, "by the galliard"; but it is evident from contemporary letters that Hatton was jealous of the favour that the Queen was showing to Oxford, and that a rivalry had developed between the two of them. This rivalry seems to have extended into the literary field, culminating in 1580 with the presentation of *Twelfth Night*, a play about the rise of an unworthy gentleman, in which Malvolio can be seen as a caricature of Christopher Hatton.

During the early 1570s Oxford made repeated requests to the Queen and Lord Burghley to be given licence to travel on the Continent, but both were opposed to the idea of foreign travel. However, in the middle of 1574, he travelled to the Continent without obtaining their permission so, on the orders of Elizabeth he was escorted back by Thomas Bedingfield. As Bertram says when he is kept at court in *All's Well That Ends Well*: "I am commanded here and kept a coil with 'too young' and 'The next year' and 'Tis too early' ", ending the passage with "By heaven, I'll steal away".

Elizabeth and Burghley must have realized that Oxford was intent on foreign travel and that they could not hold him at court for much longer, and so, on 7 January 1575, Oxford set out from London on a grand tour of the Continent, having this time obtained the permission of Elizabeth and Lord Burghley.

When he arrived in Paris in mid-March, Oxford received a letter from Burghley which confirmed that Oxford's wife Anne was pregnant, and asked Oxford therefore to return. Apparently, before Oxford had left London, he had been told by his wife Anne that she thought that she might be pregnant. It is known that Oxford had told Lord Howard and Dr Richard Masters, one of the Queen's physicians that, if his wife was pregnant, then he was not the father as he "lay not" with his wife since they were at Hampton Court together in October. There is some doubt as to whether he meant that he was not the father, or that his wife was not pregnant but, with the confirmation that she was pregnant he must have suspected that he might not have been the father. Even so, he seems to have been prepared to accept that the child could have been his own. He replied to Burghley on 17 March saying that he was glad that he was to be a father, but he did not agree that it was an "occasion to return", and that with the birth of a son, as he hoped it would be, "methinks I have the better occasion to travel".

From Paris, Oxford travelled to Strasbourg and a meeting with Johannes Sturm, or Sturmius, the director of the Strasbourg Gymnasium, and one of the leading influences on education in Europe. Oxford left Strasbourg on 26 April, spending the summer months around Padua, Genoa, and Venice.

On 24 September Oxford wrote to Burghley to say that he had borrowed 500 crowns from Master Baptista Nigrone, which he hoped Burghley would repay. He also hoped that the money had come in from the sale of his lands. He ends the letter to Burghley with "thus thanking your lordship for the good news of my wife's safe delivery". On 24 November Oxford wrote to Burghley from Padua again enquiring about the sale of his lands, and on 12 December, after receiving a remittance through Pasquino Spinola in Venice, Oxford went to Florence, Verona, and Siena. Oxford had borrowed 500 crowns from Baptista Nigrone, and received a remittance through Pasquino Spinola. In *The Taming of the Shrew*, Katherine's father is called Baptista Minola, an almost exact combination of the two names.

He again wrote to Burghley on 3 January 1576 saying "I understand the greatness of my debt and greediness of my creditors grows so dishonourable and troublesome to your Lordship, that that land of mine which in Cornwall I have appoined[sic] to be sold according to that first order for mine expenses in this travel, be gone through and withal". He also confirmed that Burghley had the authority to "sell more of my land where your Lordship shall think fittest". As Rosalind says to Jaques somewhat mockingly in *As You Like It*: "I fear you have sold your land to see other men's".

Edward Webbe in his book *The Travels of Edward Webbe*, written in 1590, remembers that the Earl of Oxford in Palermo, Sicily, "made there a challenge against all manner of persons whatsoever, and all manner of weapons, as Tournament, Barriers with horse and armour, to fight a combat with any whatsoever in the defence of his Prince and Country. For which he was highly commended, and yet no man durst be so hardy to encounter with him, so that all Italy over he is acknowledged the only Chevalier and Nobleman of England".

One of the stock characters in the Commedia dell' Arte was Graziano, a talkative Bolognese doctor, and one of his famous recitals was the Tirade of the Tournaments, a skit on the tournaments of the day. He introduced into this skit an amusing story of Milord of Oxford tilting against Alvida, Countess of Edenburg, both of them landing simultaneously face down in the dust. Gifts "out of the cupboard of antiquity" were "awarded to all the knights and amazons", Oxford "was given the horn of Astolf, paladin of Charlemagne, the magic horn to rout armies, a spear of sorts, to shake, with enchanted consequences".

Oxford returned to Paris on 31 March 1576, and there he received a letter from Burghley asking him to hasten homeward. Crossing the Channel, Oxford's ship was captured by pirates, as was Hamlet's ship when crossing the Channel to England.

When Oxford arrived in England he refused to see his wife. Burghley wrote a long, rambling, almost incomprehensible letter to the Queen, in which he seems to be saying that he does not know of any reason why Oxford should "mislike" him or his daughter, the Countess of Oxford, who "hath always used herself honestly, chastely, and lovingly towards him".

On 27 April, Oxford wrote to Burghley saying that he was determined not to accompany his wife, and that "I mean not to weary my life any more with such troubles and molestations as I have endured; nor will I, to please your Lordship only, discontent myself".

He then goes on to write, "This might have been done through private conference before, and had not needed to have been the fable of the world if you would have had the patience to have understood me; but I do not know by whom, or whose advice it was to run that course so contrary to my will or meaning that made her so disgraced to the world [and] raised suspicions openly that, with private conference, might have been more silently handled, and hath given me more greater cause to dislike".

While in Italy, Oxford had been told by Burghley that the child had been born on 2 July, but he did not learn this news until a day or two before 24 September.

It seems clear that Oxford accepted the child as his own, even though he suspected otherwise; until that is he arrived in Paris on his way back to England. There he probably learned of the rumours circulating in London to the effect that the child had not been born until September, rumours reinforced by the fact that the baptism had not been until 29 September, almost three months after the supposed date of birth, an exceptionally long delay in Elizabethan times.

Oxford was to be separated from his wife for five and a half years, returning to her only after other traumatic episodes in his life. As Angelo says in *Measure for Measure*: "Five years since there was some speech of marriage betwixt myself and her, which was broke off . . . . for that her reputation was disvalued in levity: since which time of five years I never spake with her, saw her, nor heard from her".

Lord Burghley came to believe that Oxford had been led by "the untrue reports of others" to "think unkindness in me towards him" and that "these untruths are still continued in secret reports". This may very well have been substantially correct as, soon after his return from Italy,

Oxford and several of his friends, including Lord Henry Howard, brother of the executed Duke of Norfolk, Charles Arundel, and Robert Southwell made a secret declaration to promote the advancement of the Roman Catholic religion. Some commentators see the events surrounding Oxford's separation from his wife as a plot to split Oxford from the Protestant Cecil family and return him to the Roman Catholic faith.

While on the Continent he had the freedom to go exactly where he wanted, and to do exactly what he wanted and therefore, when he returned to England, he wished to lead his own life and would not "to please your Lordship only, discontent" himself. He preferred the company of his "lewd friends" as Burghley had called them: the writers, the poets, the playwrights, the actors, and this could also have been a contributory factor in the separation from his wife and the split from the Cecil family.

Oxford had been influenced by everything Italian: Italian fashion, Italian manners, Italian religion, and the Italian theatre, and it was in the late 1570s when he wrote the early plays which have Italian settings; *The Taming of the Shrew, The Two Gentlemen of Verona, The Merchant of Venice* and, a little later, *Romeo and Juliet*.

In 1576 a group of London merchants, led by Michael Lok, engaged Martin Frobisher to find a north-west passage to the Orient. Although they failed to find the north-west passage they did return with a small piece of mineral commonly believed to contain gold. The Company of Cathay was formed and the money was raised to send a slightly larger expedition to find gold in what became known as Frobisher Bay. Elizabeth I became the leading backer, or Cathaian, of the expedition, investing £100; the Earl of Oxford invested £25. Frobisher sailed to look for gold in May 1577, returning in September with 160 tons of ore. The assay reports were inconclusive, but Lok felt confident that the ore contained silver and gold. London merchants and members of the nobility, thinking that a northern El Dorado had been found, scrambled to invest in a large expedition of fifteen ships. This time Elizabeth and Oxford invested £1000 each, but Oxford bought an additional £2000 of stock from Michael Lok, so becoming the largest investor in the expedition.

The third expedition left on a wave of enthusiasm, but returned completely unheralded, as the ore from the second expedition had proved to be worthless. Frobisher charged Michael Lok with having prior knowledge of the value of the ore, saying that he had been "a false accountant to the company" and "a cozener to my Lord of Oxford". Lok, held responsible for the losses of the investors, although he claimed to be innocent, was confined to the debtors' prison, where he eventually died.

In *The Merchant of Venice*, Michael Lok becomes Shylock; and Antonio, in bond to Shylock for 3000 ducats because of the supposed loss of his merchant ships, is Oxford, who had lost £3000 in the expedition. In 1577 Oxford sold three of his estates, in 1578 a further two, in 1579 five more, and in 1580 thirteen more, all no doubt due to the losses which he had incurred with his investments in the Cathay Company.

In July 1578 Elizabeth stopped at Audley End in Essex during a Progress to Cambridge. Gabriel Harvey, a Fellow of Trinity College, Cambridge, addressed Elizabeth's court. After eulogizing Elizabeth, Burghley, and Leicester, he paid this remarkable tribute to the Earl of Oxford who, it must be remembered, was only twenty-eight at the time. "Thy merit doth not creep along the ground, nor can it be confined within the limits of a song. It is a wonder which reaches as far as the heavenly orbs . . . . Mars will obey thee, Hermes will be thy messenger, Pallas striking her shield with her spear shaft will attend thee. For a long time past Phoebus Apollo has cultivated thy mind in the arts. English poetical measures have been sung by thee long enough. Let that Courtly Epistle more polished even than the writings of Castiglione himself – witness how greatly thou dost excel in letters. I have seen many Latin verses of thine, yea, even more English verses are extant; thou has drunk deep draughts not only of the Muses of France and Italy, but hast learned the manners of many men, and the arts of foreign countries. It was not for nothing that Sturmius himself was visited by thee: neither in France, Italy, nor Germany are any such cultivated and polished men. O thou hero worthy of renown, throw away the insignificant pen, throw away bloodless books, and writings that serve no useful purpose, now must the sword be brought into play, now is the time for thee to sharpen the spear and to handle great engines of war. On all sides men are talking of camps and of deadly weapons, war and the Furies are everywhere, and Bellona reigns supreme . . . . And what if suddenly a most powerful enemy should invade our borders? . . . . In thy breast is noble blood. Courage animates thy brow. Mars lives in thy tongue, Minerva strengthens thy right hand, Bellona reigns in thy blood, within thee burns the fire of Mars. Thine eyes flash fire, thy countenance shakes spears; who would not swear that Achilles had come to life again?"

Pallas, known as the spear-shaker because she was said to have sprung from the brow of Zeus brandishing a spear, became the patron goddess of Athens, home of the drama. In Rome the guild of poets and dramatists met at the Temple of Pallas. The Earl of Oxford was also the Viscount Bulbeck, and his coat of arms as the Viscount was a lion brandishing or shaking a broken spear which, having been broken in battle, symbolically shows that he had fought courageously.

So this address by Harvey combines the image of Pallas, the spear-shaker, attending Oxford, the poet and dramatist, with the implied image of the Bulbeck lion shaking a broken spear to symbolize Oxford as a courageous defender of his country.

One of the earliest of English novels was *Euphues: the Anatomy of Wyt* by John Lyly, published in December 1578. Six months later a sequel appeared, *Euphues and his England.* Dedicating the second book to the Earl of Oxford, Lyly says that the first book *The Anatomy of Wyt* had been "sent to a nobleman to nurse for a year, so that wheresoever he wander he hath his nurse's name in his forehead". By this time Lyly was Oxford's secretary, and it should not be too difficult to imagine who this nobleman might have been. Lyly is supposed to have written eight plays, all of which were first printed without an author's name. Subsequent printings during his lifetime did however bear his name.

In 1583 Oxford acquired the lease of Blackfriars Theatre, which he transferred to his secretary, John Lyly. Blackfriars was associated with boy players, and all but one of Lyly's plays are described on the title-page as having been presented by boy players, presumably at the Blackfriars Theatre where Lyly was the manager and Oxford the patron.

Gabriel Harvey called Lyly Oxford's "minion secretary", and in 1593 he said that Lyly was the "fiddlestick of Oxford, the babble of London"; but it has been argued that he meant the University of Oxford and not the Earl of Oxford. However, Lyly wrote nothing before his association with the Earl of Oxford, and nothing after his association with the Earl of Oxford ended in 1592.

There must have been some rivalry between Oxford and Philip Sidney from about 1569, if not before, when Lord Burghley, then William Cecil, was trying to find a husband for his daughter Anne. By the late 1570s their rivalry had become literary. Leaders of two styles of writing, Oxford headed the newly arisen Euphuist movement, and Sidney the Romanticists.

In September 1579 the two quarrelled on a tennis court, not about English verse, but, as reported, because Oxford tried to eject Sidney so that he, Oxford, could use it himself. From this incident anti-Oxfordian academics have interpreted that Oxford must have been arrogant and insolent with everyone throughout the whole of his life. Apparently Sidney challenged Oxford to a duel, but Oxford did not take this seriously. The Queen rebuked Sidney for ignoring the difference in degree between Earls and Gentlemen. The incident, as reported, does not show Oxford in a particularly good light, but we do not have Oxford's side of the story. Or do we?

Philip Sidney is caricatured in *The Merry Wives of Windsor* as Slender; in *Twelfth Night* as Sir Andrew Aguecheek, who is incapable of fighting a duel with someone whom the audience knows to be a woman disguised as a man; and in *Love's Labour's Lost* as Boyet, little boy, which is similar to Oxford's calling Sidney a "puppy", as he was heard to do during the quarrel on the tennis court.

The quarrel could not have been as significant to the two participants as the academics imagine it to have been, because they were jousting together as the defendants against the challengers Lord Arundel and Sir William Drury in a tournament in January 1581.

In 1580 Oxford had an affair with Anne Vavasor, then about twenty years old, and a Gentlewoman of the Queen's Bedchamber. The Vavasors were one of the most important Roman Catholic families of the day and, as Lord Henry Howard was a cousin of both Anne Vavasor and the Earl of Oxford, it has been suggested that he engineered the affair to widen the rift between Oxford and the Cecil family.

Very little is known about Anne Vavasor, but Oxfordians believe her to be the model for Rosaline in *Love's Labour's Lost*, Beatrice in *Much Ado About Nothing*, and the dark lady of the sonnets because her portrait shows her to have been a woman with dark eyes and dark hair.

Towards the end of the year an incident happened that is clouded in mystery. Apparently Oxford denounced Henry Howard and Charles Arundel as enemies of the state, revealing that they had been plotting with Catholic powers. Although Oxford had made a secret declaration to promote the advancement of the Roman Catholic religion he was not prepared to go so far as to depose Elizabeth to achieve those aims. He remained the same man who, while in Italy, had challenged "all manner of persons whatsoever" "in the defence of his Prince and Country".

Three years later, in 1583, a more substantial plot to depose Elizabeth called for a French force led by the Duke of Guise to invade England, release Mary, Queen of Scots, and re-establish the Roman Catholic religion. The plan failed because Francis Throckmorton, under surveillance by Walsinghan's secret service, revealed all he knew when put on the rack. Documents later confirmed details of the plan. The conspirators arrested included Henry Howard, who was imprisoned and later put under house arrest, never again to regain Elizabeth's trust. Philip Howard, Earl of Arundel, was arrested trying to leave the country, and died in prison in 1595, having been convicted of high treason for sympathizing with the Spanish Armada. Charles Arundel managed to escape to the Continent.

In March 1581 Anne Vavasor gave birth to a boy who was to become known as Edward Vere. Walsingham writes, "The Gentlewoman the selfsame night she was delivered was conveyed out of the house and the next day committed to the Tower". He also says, "Her Majesty is greatly grieved with the accident". It was, of course, Elizabeth who had had them committed to the Tower. Oxford was also committed to the Tower until 8 June, but he remained under house arrest until the end of the year.

These events form the basic plot of *Measure for Measure*, in which Claudio and his mistress Juliet are imprisoned because Juliet is pregnant.

After five years with his Catholic friends, whom he had denounced as enemies of the State, and an affair with the Catholic Anne Vavasor which had resulted in the loss of freedom for nine months, Oxford returned to his wife and the Protestant Cecil family some time around Christmas 1581.

It seems that he felt able to acknowledge his wife's child Elizabeth as being his own, but I think that he had always been prepared to do this; it was the fact that his wife had been 'disgraced to the world' that had caused the separation.

Oxford started writing a series of plays, in each of which a husband suspects his wife of being unfaithful, only to find out later that he has been mistaken. These plays include *The Merry Wives of Windsor, All's Well That Ends Well, Othello* and *The Winter's Tale*. The plays probably had the effect of restoring his wife's reputation with those who knew that he had written them, as in each of the plays the wife proves to be innocent, whereas the husband's jealous actions show him to have been the real guilty party.

After their reconciliation the Earl and Countess of Oxford had two daughters, Bridget and Susan; a third daughter died in early childhood, and a newly-born son also died.

Less than three months after their reconciliation a sword fight occurred between the Earl of Oxford and Thomas Knyvet, a member of the Privy Chamber who had just been made Keeper of Westminster Palace. Knyvet was an uncle of Anne Vavasor and as such a relative of the Howards. It is presumed that the sword fight arose from Oxford's affair with Anne Vavasor and, as Knyvet must have felt himself to have been the aggrieved party it seems logical to suppose that he was also the aggressive party. Oxford was wounded in the leg and remained lame for the rest of his life. As he wrote in sonnet 89: "Speak of my lameness and straight I will halt", and again in sonnet 37: "So I, made lame by Fortune's dearest spite" and "So that I am not lame, poor, nor despised".

Over the next twelve months five or six sword fights broke out on the streets of London between the followers of Oxford and Knyvet. Oxford himself is not reported to have been involved in any of the fights except the first, when he was probably attacked by Knyvet. At least two people, possibly three, were killed in the sword fights, one of them by Knyvet himself.

These 'brabbles and frays' as Burghley called them became source material for the feud between the Montagues and the Capulets in *Romeo and Juliet*.

In a letter which Burghley wrote to the Earl of Leicester, he says that "my Lord of Oxford . . . . hath, I confess, forgotten his duty to God". It seems that Oxford's involvement with the Howards, his affair with Anne Vavasor, and the feud with Thomas Knyvet had caused him to become disillusioned with all religion.

Oxford was back under the ever-watchful eye of Lord Burghley and, in October 1584, he was told that Burghley had been using one of Oxford's men, Amis, to inform Burghley of Oxford's situation. Oxford wrote to Burghley on 30 October: "I think it very strange that your Lordship should enter into that course towards me . . . . But I pray my Lord, leave that course, for I mean not to be your ward, nor your child. I serve Her Majesty, and I am that I am, and by alliance near to your Lordship, but free, and scorn to be offered that injury to think I am so weak of government as to be ruled by servants, or not able to govern myself. If your Lordship take and follow this course you deceive yourself, and make me take another course that I have not yet thought of".

The phrase "I am that I am", is used in sonnet 121,

"No, I am that I am, and they that level
At my abuses reckon up their own"

and would have come from Oxford's Geneva Bible, which has recently been rediscovered in the Folger Shakespeare Library, Washington.

The phrase "make me take another course that I have not yet thought of", was to find its way into *King Lear*: "I will do such things, what they are yet, I know not".

Oxford says in the letter: "I serve Her Majesty", but how did he serve Her Majesty?

In March 1584 towns in the Low Countries were falling to the Duke of Parma and Sturmius appealed to Elizabeth to send an English force, to be led by the Earl of Oxford, or the Earl of Leicester, or Philip Sidney. On 29 August Oxford left for the Low Countries in command of the English horse. In September the Earl of Leicester was given overall command and, by 21 October, Oxford was back in England.

This was one of only two known official appointments that the Earl of Oxford ever received in the service of Her Majesty, neither of them lasting for more than a few weeks.

Oxford's service to Her Majesty may well have been as one of the writers of the plays presented at court and as the patron of his theatrical companies which toured the country.

Early in 1580 Oxford had taken over the Earl of Warwick's company; in 1583 he acquired the lease of the Blackfriars Theatre used by his own boys' company; and in 1584 he had taken over the Earl of Worcester's company.

Oxford's theatrical activities became even more of a drain on his resources than the Cathay Company and his continental travels. Between 1581 and 1584 he sold a further nineteen estates, and continued to sell off his land and estates for the rest of the decade. In 1583 Burghley informed the Queen of the Earl and Countess of Oxford's relative poverty, saying that they had only three servants; and, still on the same theme, in 1587 he wrote to Walsingham saying "No enemy I have can envy me this match; for thereby neither honour nor land nor goods shall come to their children".

It must have been around this time, 1585 or 1586, when Oxford wrote *Timon of Athens*, the story of a noble Athenian who, through his munificence, is reduced to such poverty that he has to dig for roots and live in a cave in the woods.

On 26 June 1586 Elizabeth I authorized "the Treasurer and Chamberlain of our Exchequer . . . . to deliver and pay . . . . unto Our right trusty Cousin the Earl of Oxford . . . . the sum of One Thousand Pounds good and lawful money of England. The same to be yearly delivered and paid unto Our said Cousin at four terms of the year by even portions, and so to be continued unto him during Our pleasure, or until such time as he shall be by Us otherwise provided for to be in some manner relieved; at what time Our pleasure is that this payment of One Thousand Pounds yearly to Our said Cousin in manner above specified shall cease".

This annuity of one thousand pounds, the equivalent of more than a million pounds today, was a larger grant than anyone else received in the whole country, with the exception of James VI of Scotland, the Master of the Posts, and the Lord President of the North. Oxford drew on this grant for the rest of his life, as James renewed the annuity when he came to the throne. Again, what service had Oxford rendered to Her Majesty that could justify such an astonishing amount? A service which would also be appreciated by James I? It could only have been for the upkeep of his theatrical companies which toured the country with the plays he had written: plays which had the effect of uniting the nation behind Elizabeth I against the threats made internally with the support of foreign powers. These were the history plays which showed the devastation and turmoil of civil wars: *Richard II, Henry IV, Henry VI, Richard III, Macbeth* and *Julius Caesar. Henry V* would have been written to unite the nation against the threats from foreign powers, especially at a time when the Spanish were preparing to invade England with the Armada.

The Earl of Oxford was one of the forty-two commissioners who sat under Lord Burghley at the trial of Mary, Queen of Scots in October 1586. Unlike some Oxfordians I do not think that the man who believed in one nation under Elizabeth I would have had much sympathy for Mary, Queen of Scots.

The Spanish Armada sailed for England on 20 May 1588 but, delayed by storms, had to put into port, and was eventually sighted on 19 July off the western coast of England.

On 5 June 1588, Anne, Countess of Oxford died from a fever. The Earl is not reported as being at his wife's interment at Westminster Abbey, but a cousin and his sister Mary were present. Oxford would have been preparing his ship the "Edward Bonaventure" to meet the Spanish Armada. He had bought this ship in 1581 to go on trading expeditions led by Edward Fenton.

The Spanish were planning to use the Armada to clear the English Channel of English ships so that the Duke of Parma could cross the Channel without any opposition;

but the English fleet outmanoeuvred the Armada as they sailed up the Channel towards Calais. On 27 July, the Earl of Leicester, writing to Lord Burghley, says of Oxford: "I trust he be free to go to the enemy, for he seems most willing to hazard his life in this quarrel"; but Oxford was not free, as he had been appointed governor of Harwich. The next day the English fleet attacked the Armada.

If the Armada had been successful and the Duke of Parma had invaded England, then Harwich might have been of some strategic importance but, as the Armada was defeated, Harwich was well clear of any action. It may well be that Elizabeth, in transferring Oxford to Harwich the day before the English attacked the Armada, did so to protect him from danger.

On 24 November 1588, following a royal procession to St. Paul's, a thanksgiving service celebrated victory over the Spanish Armada.

> 'The noble Earl of Oxford then High Chamberlain
>   of England
> Rode right before Her Majesty his bonnet
>   in his hand".

The Queen was brought through the long west aisle under a "rich canopy" carried by six dignitaries, one of whom was "The Lord Great Chamberlain of England", the Earl of Oxford. Sonnet 125 begins: "Were't aught to me I bore the canopy".

The Arte of English Poesie attributed to George Puttenham was published in 1589, and in it he writes: "Among the nobility or gentry . . . . it is to come to pass that they have no courage to write & if they have are loath to be known of their skill. So as I know very many notable gentlemen in the court that have written commendably, and suppressed it again, or else suffered it to be published without their own name to it: as if it were a discredit for a gentleman, to seem learned". Later in the same book he writes: "And in Her Majesty's time that now is are sprung up another crew of courtly makers,

Noblemen and Gentlemen of Her Majesty's own servants, who have written excellently well as it would appear if their doings could be found out and made public with the rest, of which number is first that noble gentleman, Edward Earl of Oxford".

Before Oxford could marry Anne Cecil in 1571, he had to purchase his freedom to marry from the Court of Wards. The full price had never been paid; therefore in 1589, the year after Anne's death, her father Lord Burghley, Master of the Court of Wards, sued the Earl of Oxford for this debt, and some of Oxford's lands were seized and held for payment.

By 1590 Oxford had sold almost all of his lands and estates and may even have had some difficulty in finding somewhere to live.

It is supposed that Shakespeare wrote *As You Like It* at Billesley Hall near Stratford-upon-Avon. If this is correct, then it must have been the Earl of Oxford who was writing there sometime around 1589, as the house was owned by Thomas Trussel, a relative of Oxford's grandmother Elizabeth Trussel, who had married the fifteenth Earl of Oxford.

Another house near to the River Avon and the Forest of Arden where Oxford may have lived at that time was Bilton Manor near Rugby, a property belonging to Elizabeth Trussel which eventually passed to the Earl of Oxford. Elizabeth's family coat-of-arms included a trussel or candleholder, which is probably why Romeo says: "I am proverb'd with a grandsire phrase; I'll be a candleholder and look on".

In December 1591 Oxford handed over to Lord Burghley his hereditary seat of Hedingham Castle, to be held in trust for Oxford's three daughters. Oxford must have drawn upon this episode in his life when he was writing *King Lear*, the story of a king who divides his kingdom into three parts to give to his three daughters. The Fool tells Lear that a snail has a house to put his head in, "not to give away to his daughters"; "head in" being a pun on Hedingham.

Towards the end of 1591, or the beginning of 1592, Oxford married Elizabeth Trentham, one of the Queen's Maids of Honour and the daughter of Sir Thomas Trentham, a Staffordshire landowner. The couple settled in the village of Stoke Newington, and it was there on 24 February 1593 that their son and heir, Henry, was born.

The Earl and Countess of Oxford moved in 1596 to King's Place, Hackney, where the Earl spent the rest of his life. The house had been bought by the Countess.

On 16 April 1594, Lord Strange, the fifth Earl of Derby, died, leaving his theatre company to his wife. On 5 June, the patronage of the Lord Chamberlain, Henry, Lord Hunsdon, was obtained and the company became known as the Lord Chamberlain's Men. On 26 January 1595, the Earl of Oxford's eldest daughter, Elizabeth, married William Stanley, the sixth Earl of Derby.

Lord Hunsdon's career comprised a long series of military and political offices, which did not allow him to reside regularly at court. The elderly politician Lord Cobham succeeded Lord Hunsdon and, in March 1596, the second Lord Hunsdon, also preoccupied with military and diplomatic duties, became Lord Chamberlain. Far from being a patron of the theatre, the second Lord Hunsdon actually opposed the opening of James Burbage's new theatre at Blackfriars in 1596.

"The Lord Chamberlain's was the best organized and most favoured and successful acting company in England", writes Charlton Ogburn Jr., and it is most unlikely that any of these men could have had the time or the inclination to have been responsible for such a prestigious company. Although the patron of the company was nominally the Lord Chamberlain, it is far more likely that the man responsible for the success of the company would have been the Lord Great Chamberlain, the Earl of Oxford, probably assisted by his son-in-law the sixth Earl of Derby, whose elder brother, the fifth Earl of Derby, had formerly been the company's patron.

Orthodox Shakespearean academics say that Shakespeare was the resident playwright of the Lord

Chamberlain's Men. They also say that before Shakespeare joined the Lord Chamberlain's Men, he may have been a member of the Earl of Pembroke's Men, as they were in possession of some of his early plays.

On 8 September 1597, the Earl of Oxford wrote to Lord Burghley to say that all parties were agreeable to the proposed marriage of his daughter Bridget and William Herbert, the eldest son of the Earl and Countess of Pembroke. However, the marriage did not take place.

In 1605, the year after Oxford died, his youngest daughter, Susan, married the second son of the Earl and Countess of Pembroke, Philip Herbert, Earl of Montgomery. Incidentally, Philip Herbert was probably named after his uncle Sir Philip Sidney, whose sister Mary was Countess of Pembroke.

In 1623 the First Folio of the works of William Shakespeare was published, and was dedicated "To the most noble and Incomparable Paire of Brethren, William Earle of Pembroke . . . . and Philip Earle of Montgomery", presumably because they had paid for the publication of the First Folio. So the Earl of Oxford's son-in-law, Philip Herbert, and his brother, William Herbert, who had been engaged to Oxford's daughter Bridget, were responsible for the publication of the First Folio of works by William Shakespeare.

Lord Burghley died on 4 August 1598, aged 78, leaving an enormous estate which included 298 separate properties.

A month later Francis Meres's *Palladis Tamia* was entered in the Stationers' Register, and for the first time William Shakespeare is mentioned as the author of twelve plays which had previously been anonymous. Until 1598, Shakespeare had been known only as the author of two narrative poems *Venus and Adonis* and *The Rape of Lucrece*.

In 1598 a decree of the Privy Council limited to two the number of theatrical companies allowed to play in London: the Lord Chamberlain's Men and the Lord Admiral's Men, but in September 1599 a third company was allowed, which was probably the Earl of Oxford's company.

In June 1600 Oxford sought the help of Sir Robert Cecil, Lord Burghley's son who had become the Queen's Secretary of State, in obtaining the Governorship of Jersey; but in vain. Six months later he again sought Cecil's help, this time in obtaining the Presidency of Wales, again without success.

On 7 February 1601, the Earl of Essex led an uprising through the streets of London. On the eve of the uprising the Earl of Southampton arranged for the Lord Chamberlain's Men to enact the "old play" *Richard II*, "in the hope that the play scene of the deposition of the king might excite the citizens of London to countenance their rebellious design". However, it seems that a performance was not given. During the uprising a small group of Essex's followers put up a brief defence, but they then surrendered and were arrested. At the trial of the Earl of Essex and the Earl of Southampton, the Earl of Oxford was the senior nobleman of the twenty-five on the tribunal. Essex and Southampton were found guilty of treason and condemned to death, but Southampton's sentence was commuted to life imprisonment.

An investigation was held into the performance of *Richard II* scheduled for the eve of the uprising, but no one mentioned the author of the play; no one mentioned William Shakespeare. Six months later Elizabeth I, who must have been thinking about the play's connection with the uprising, was reported as saying: "I am Richard II, know ye not that?" and "He that will forget God will also forget his benefactors". Oxfordians believe that "He that will forget God" refers to the author of the play, the Earl of Oxford and, of course, one of his benefactors, in fact the most important, was Elizabeth I.

In 1602 the Earl of Oxford's Men were combined with the Earl of Worcester's Men and allowed to play in London at the Boar's Head.

Queen Elizabeth died on 24 March 1603. Shortly afterwards Oxford wrote to Robert Cecil, saying: "I cannot but find great grief in myself to remember the Mistress which we have lost, under whom both you and myself from our greenest years have been in a manner brought up . . . . In this common shipwreck mine is above all the rest, who least regarded though often comforted of all her followers, she hath left to try my fortune among the alterations of time and chance, either without sail whereby to take advantage of any prosperous gale, or with anchor to ride till the storm be overpast". He then goes on to ask "what course is devised by you of the Council and the rest of the Lords concerning our duties to the King's Majesty . . . . and what order is resolved on amongst you either for the attending or meeting of His Majesty; for by reasons of my infirmity I cannot come amongst you as often as I wish". The Earl of Oxford attended Parliament only nine times after 1589, and not at all after 1597.

Within three weeks of his accession, James I released the Earl of Southampton from the Tower. Even before his coronation, James I had granted to the Earl of Oxford his petition for the custody of the Forest of Essex and the Keepership of Havering House. In his petition Oxford wrote: "mine ancestors have possessed the same, almost since the time of William Conqueror, and at that time – which was the 12th year of Henry VIII – the King took it for the term of his life, from my grandfather; since which time, what by the alterations of Princes and Wardships, I have been kept from my rightful possession . . . . Twice in my time it had passage by law and judgement was to have been passed on my side, where of Her Majesty, the late Queen, being advertised, with assured promise and words of a Prince to restore it herself unto me, caused me to let fall the suit. But so it was she was not so ready to perform her word, as I was too ready to believe it".

In the first month after his coronation, James I renewed the Earl of Oxford's annuity and reappointed him to the Royal Privy Council. James I took over the patronage of the Lord Chamberlain's Men, who now became known as the King's Men; Queen Anne took over the patronage of the Earl of Oxford's and the Earl of

Worcester's combined company; and Prince Henry took over the patronage of the Lord Admiral's Men.

The Earl of Oxford's infirmity may have been his lameness, but it also may have been a weakness caused by ill health. Just before he died he arranged for his son-in-law Francis, Lord Norris of Rycote and his cousin, Sir Francis Vere, to share custody of the Forest of Essex, and he made his cousin the guardian of his son Henry. The Earl of Oxford died from the plague on 24 June 1604, aged 54, and was buried in the Church of St. Augustine, Hackney.

In the winter of 1604-1605, the first that the King and Queen had spent in winter because of the plague, *Othello*, *The Merry Wives of Windsor*, *Measure for Measure*, *Love's Labour's Lost*, *Henry V*, and *The Merchant of Venice*, twice, were presented at court. This would have been the first opportunity to present a series of plays in memory of the Earl of Oxford.

In 1608 the Countess of Oxford sold her house King's Place to Fulke Greville, Lord Brooke, who renamed it Brooke House. It was demolished in 1955.

The Countess of Oxford's will bequeathed an unspecified amount to be paid quarterly "to my dombe man". These payments were probably to William Shakspere, who had been receiving them since about 1597, when he bought New Place, the second largest house in Stratford-upon-Avon.

On 25 November 1612, six weeks before she died, the Countess of Oxford wrote: "I joyfully commit my body to the earth from whence it was taken, desiring to be buried in the Church of Hackney, within the County of Middlesex, as near unto the body of my said dear and noble Lord and husband as may be . . . . Only I will that there be in the said Church erected for us a tomb fitting our degree".

There is however a possibility, reported by the Earl of Oxford's cousin, Percival Golding, that the Earl of Oxford may have been reburied in the de Vere tomb in Westminster Abbey, along with his cousins Francis and Horace, and his son Henry.

Over the next four years I read Charlton Ogburn Jr.'s book several times, as well as frequently dipping into it whenever I wanted to refer to an event in the Earl of Oxford's life.

I also consulted *The Seventeenth Earl of Oxford, from Contemporary Documents* (1928), a biography by Bernard M. Ward. Although Ward's book delves into the Earl of Oxford's life in great detail, he does not claim that the Earl of Oxford was Shakespeare, saying that that aspect of the Earl's life is beyond the scope of his book. Therefore, as Charlton Ogburn quotes extensively from Ward's book, and as his is more broadly based than Ward's book, I feel that Ogburn's book is the most complete book on Oxford's life.

I also read some conventional biographies of Shakespeare written by orthodox academics who believe that Shakespeare was William Shakspere of Stratford-upon-Avon. Charlton Ogburn's assertion that Stratfordian biographies are predominately supposition based on very thin evidence and very few facts proved to be glaringly obvious.

To take just one very simple example. Shakespeare was the greatest dramatist of his age, or of any age, writing tragedies, comedies, histories, and narrative poems; in so doing, he was greatly influenced by the classics, particularly Ovid. The supposition is that William Shakspere must have been a highly educated man, and therefore must have received his education from Stratford Grammar School. This supposition can be maintained only because there are no surviving records from Stratford Grammar School.

The Stratfordians cannot state that William Shakspere went to a university, because there are surviving university records which do not mention a William Shakspere. So, Stratfordian biographers have to believe that William Shakspere must have received the whole of his education at Stratford Grammar School, learning everything that he would need to know to become the world's greatest playwright before he left the school at fourteen. After receiving this education, he apparently did nothing to utilize it for a further twelve or thirteen years, when he is supposed to have written his first play.

There are no records of William Shakspere ever having been to school for even one day in the whole of his life. But why should he have gone to school? His parents did not go to school, and were illiterate. His daughters did not go to school, and were also illiterate.

After one has read about the Earl of Oxford, the biographies of the Stratford man have a very hollow ring indeed. After reading about Oxford, Shakespeare is no longer a blank, almost anonymous figure, but a fully rounded person who can be clearly visualized in the mind's eye: a man with many good qualities, who was prepared to give up everything that he had for the sake of his art; a man who found some happiness in his life, but who had many disappointments and great misfortune.

I tried to discover more about the Earl of Oxford, but unfortunately, apart from Charlton Ogburn's book, I found no other books on the market. Oxford is mentioned in biographies of Elizabeth I, but these are only disparaging references to his arrogance and intolerable behaviour. Each time I went into a bookshop I expected to find a new book about the Earl of Oxford that might follow on from Ogburn's book, but found nothing. I saw many books about Shakespeare on the shelves, almost a new book every week, each of them trying to create a life and a personality for William Shakspere from nothing more than supposition and conjecture.

It has been thought that Shakespeare wrote *A Midsummer Night's Dream* for an aristocratic wedding. Some scholars believe that the play had been written by Shakespeare, meaning Shakspere, for the wedding of the Earl of Derby. Other scholars believe that Shakspere wrote the play for the wedding of the Earl and Countess of Pembroke's son, William Herbert. Do they not know that the Earl of Derby had married the Earl of Oxford's eldest daughter Elizabeth, and that two years later a proposal of marriage had been made between William Herbert and the Earl of Oxford's second daughter, Bridget? It was much more likely that the Earl of Oxford had written *A Midsummer Night's Dream* for the wedding of his daughter to the Earl of Derby; or, even though he did not marry Bridget de Vere, for the wedding of William Herbert, the son of his friends and fellow theatrical patrons the Earl and Countess of Pembroke. It seems that the Stratfordians try to bring William Shakspere closer and closer towards the aristocratic circle of the Earl of Oxford, whilst at the same time they refuse to consider the possibility that the Earl of Oxford could have been Shakespeare.

It also occurred to me that these orthodox academics were trying to do exactly the same thing to Charlton Ogburn's book that they had done to J. Thomas Looney's book in the 'twenties and 'thirties. They could not rebuff Charlton Ogburn's assertions by argument, because they would lose hands down, so they ignored Ogburn's book with the hope that it would eventually fade away and be forgotten.

Bearing this in mind I had for some time been thinking about writing a play based on Ogburn's book, which would publicize the fact that the Earl of Oxford was Shakespeare. Unfortunately, I had been unable to come up with a format for the play, but suddenly, in a moment of inspiration, the format came to me.

I should write the play from the Earl of Oxford's point of view. He would be in his study, set to the side of the stage, late at night, a few days before he died, and thinking about whether he had put enough of himself into his plays for future generations to realize that he had been Shakespeare, or whether they would believe that a grain merchant from Stratford-upon-Avon had written his plays. He thinks back to the main events of his life, which are presented in the centre of the stage and, as these events are being acted out, the audience can see the similarity between a play based on the life of the Earl of Oxford and the plays of Shakespeare.

I immediately realized that if I were to write such a play, with the character of the Earl of Oxford speaking solo for much of the time, I should have to know absolutely everything that there is to know about him.

I had already established that Ogburn's was currently the most informative book on Oxford's life, but I felt I should know something more than this, something that only the Earl of Oxford would have known about. Therefore, there was only one other place that I could look to obtain further information. I had to read the whole of Shakespeare, and differentiate between the Earl of Oxford's creative writing, which came from his imagination, and his personal writing, which would include his thoughts, opinions, and comments.

II

Wordplay in the Drama

On reading the plays I noticed that Shakespeare uses the words true and truth very often, and that his characters are frequently drawn into conversations about being true and being truthful. He also, very often, uses words and phrases that are associated with true and truth, such as by my troth, forsooth, and soothsayer.

The reason for this is that the Earl of Oxford's family motto was: 'Vero Nihil Verius', which Ogburn translated as: 'Nothing truer than truth'. This Latin motto was chosen originally because the words form a pun on the family name of Vere. Before arriving in England with William the Conqueror the family came from Ver near Bayeux, and at that time the family name was probably pronounced de Ver. So the first three letters of 'vero' and 'verius' are the name Ver or Vere.

I was quite thrilled to realize that Oxford was using the words 'true' and 'truth' far more often than necessary, so that his audience would constantly hear two of the three words from his motto. It would have been a kind of joke between himself and those members of his audience who knew that he was the author.

During those early days of reading the plays, I also

noticed how often Shakespeare used the exclamation 'O'; again, far more often than is necessary. 'O' would, of course, stand for Oxford or Oxenford, the name that Edward de Vere used when he signed his name. Again it occurred to me that this was a joke for the inner circle of those who knew the truth, the repetition of the letter 'O' signifying that Oxford had written the plays.

Ogburn had found a similar joke in *Romeo and Juliet*, when Benvolio says: "Here comes Romeo", and Mercutio replies: "Without his roe, like a dried herring". The hidden joke is that Romeo without his 'roe', or 'ro', is 'meo'; meaning 'me O', 'me Oxenford'.

Other puns found by Ogburn include those on Malvolio and Benvolio. In *Twelfth Night*, Malvolio is a caricature of Christopher Hatton, and in Latin 'mal' means evil, 'vol' means will. Therefore: evil will to io, or E.O., Edward Oxenford. Similarly, Benvolio would therefore mean: good will to io, or E.O., Edward Oxenford.

The most important pun that Ogburn had found concerns Arthur Brooke. All Shakespearean academics agree that the source material for *Romeo and Juliet* was a poem called *The Tragicall Historye of Romeus and Juliet*, written in 1562 by Arthur Brooke.

The Earl of Oxford's second title was Viscount Bulbeck, and a beck is defined as a brook or mountain stream. So that brooke is an alternative word for beck. If the sound of Ar in Arthur is given the letter R, then the word becomes Rthur; the word rother or ruther means, according to the *Oxford English Dictionary*, appertaining to oxen. A bull or Bul would be appertaining to oxen, and therefore Arthur Brooke can be seen as a pun on Bulbeck. Arthur Brooke is also a secondary pun on Oxenford, as Arthur is clearly a pun on oxen, a ford being a shallow place where a river or stream may be crossed, so associated with a brook.

This pun does not show that the Earl of Oxford was Shakespeare, but only that the Earl of Oxford was Arthur Brooke, and that he wrote *The Tragicall Historye of Romeus and Juliet* when he was twelve years old.

However, in *The Merry Wives of Windsor*, whenever the character Ford goes to meet Falstaff, he disguises himself and changes his name to Brook. This shows that Shakespeare associated a ford with a brook, just as Oxford had associated a ford with a brook when he was twelve years old.

Reading the plays I also began to find puns on the names of characters. It will be remembered that Claudio in *Measure for Measure* is imprisoned because his mistress is pregnant, just as Oxford was imprisoned for the same reason. When he was released Oxford was wounded in a sword-fight with Sir Thomas Knyvet and made lame for the rest of his life. In Latin 'claudeo' means to be lame; so the imprisoned Claudio in *Measure for Measure* is also the lame E.O.

In *The Comedy of Errors* there are two identical servants, both called Dromio, who spend the whole of the play running here, there, and everywhere. Drom is from the Greek meaning a runner, and so Dromio is the runner E.O. or the runner to E.O. Antipholus, the name of the two identical masters of the two identical Dromios, is usually pronounced as if it were a Greek name, but if it is pronounced as two separate words with the stress on the 'o' in pholus, it would be: anti pholus; which is a pun on anti false, and of course anti false means true. So Antipholus is anti false meaning true, indicating the Earl of Oxford; and Dromio, the servant to Antipholus, is the runner to E.O.

Another group of puns revolve around words like ever, never, very; all containing the name Ver, and therefore indicating Vere. In sonnet 76 Shakespeare writes: "Why write I still all one, ever the same". This not only means "always the same", but also, "E.Ver, the same". The sonnet was written by Edward de Vere, the same Earl of Oxford.

In *The Winter's Tale* (I.i.) Hermione says to Polixenes: "You'll stay?", to which Polixenes replies: "No madam".

Hermione: Nay but you will?
Polixenes: I may not verily.

Hermione: Verily! . . . . Verily, you shall not
go: a lady's 'Verily' 's as potent as a lord's.
Will you go yet? Force me to keep you as a
prisoner. Not like a guest; . . . .
How say you? My prisoner? or my guest? by
your dread 'Verily', One of them you shall be.

Repetition of the word 'verily' would again convey to the
audience that it was de Vere who had written the play,
but in this passage 'verily' does not only mean 'truly', it
also means 'Verely', 'like de Vere'. "How saw you? My prisoner? or my guest? by your dread 'Verily' one of them you
shall be". Edward de Vere was imprisoned and then kept
under house arrest for a further six months; so, like de
Vere, Polixenes will be either Hermione's prisoner or kept
in her house as her guest.

This passage is not a coincidence. When I found this
pun I think I realized for the first time that Edward de
Vere had used certain words to convey the message to the
audience that he has written the plays. I remember thinking at the time that if I could find twenty or thirty of
these puns it would be a solid connection between the
words in the plays of Shakespeare and the Earl of Oxford,
showing that de Vere had actually written the words of
Shakespeare, not merely the circumstantial evidence of
connecting events in Oxford's life with the dramatization
of these events in the Shakespeare plays. However, these
twenty or thirty puns which I was hoping to find were to
pale into insignificance when compared to what I was to
find a few months later.

In *The Winter's Tale* Leontes suspects that Polixenes
is having an affair with his wife, Hermione; likewise in
Othello, Othello suspects that Michael Cassio is having an
affair with his wife Desdemona. The names of Cassio and
Polixenes suggested to me a pun on the mythological
twins Castor and Pollux. Was this a pun with a hidden
meaning? If so, did it mean that the Earl of Oxford knew
that his wife had had an affair with someone who was a
twin?

In *The Merry Wives of Windsor* Fenton is given the social standing, and the general characteristics, of the Earl of Oxford, and at the end of the play Fenton marries Anne. This would have had the effect of identifying this happy couple as the Earl and Countess of Oxford. Ogburn suggests that Fenton was given this name as a tribute to Geoffrey Fenton, who had dedicated one of his books to the Countess of Oxford. However, it suggested to me that the character had been given this name because de Vere was acknowledging that someone called Fenton was, or had been, his wife's true love.

Edward Fenton was the captain of the Earl of Oxford's ship the "Edward Bonaventure". Were Edward and Geoffrey Fenton related? If so, were they twins?

The *Dictionary of National Biography* states that Geoffrey and Edward Fenton were brothers, Geoffrey being born about 1539, and Edward in 1550. It seemed to me that Geoffrey Fenton would probably have been too old to have had an affair with Anne, the Countess of Oxford, and although Edward Fenton was the same age as de Vere, it seemed unlikely that de Vere would have employed him as his captain of the 'Edward Bonaventure' knowing that he had had an affair with his wife Anne.

However, the entry for Edward Fenton in the *Dictionary of National Biography* states that there was a third brother called James. The reference says that James Fenton was murdered on 10 June 1579. I wrote to the *Dictionary of National Biography*, but they did not have any additional details about James Fenton. The church registers of Sturton-le-Steeple, the parish in which the Fentons were born, date only from 1638, and there is no record of earlier details. Therefore, unless there is some information hidden elsewhere, which seems unlikely, it is no longer possible to ascertain whether Edward and James Fenton were twins. Although the search had come to a dead end, it did seem to me that James Fenton, rather than Edward Fenton, had been Anne's lover; that one of the reasons why the Earl of Oxford had returned to his wife was because James had died; and that the name

of Fenton in *The Merry Wives of Windsor* was an acknowl-
edgement that James Fenton had been Anne's true love.

At the beginning of *Cymbeline* (II.i.) Cloten relates to
two Lords the story of a quarrel that he had when he was
playing bowls, saying: "I had a hundred pounds on't; and
then a whoreson jackanapes must take me up for swearing, as if I borrowed my oaths of him, and might not
spend them at my pleasure . . . . When a gentleman is disposed to swear, it is not for any standers-by
to curtail his oaths, ha? . . . . Whoreson dog! I
give him satisfaction? Would he had been one on my rank!
. . . . I had rather not be so noble as I am".
These remarks are interspersed with asides from the second Lord, who believes that Cloten is a fool.

So this passage would appear to be Oxford's side of
the story of the quarrel on the tennis court, only the game
has been changed and the second Lord is used so that, by
mocking Cloten, Oxford is also mocking himself. From the
two versions of the quarrel that are already known, a
third can be added and we obtain a more realistic picture
of the quarrel. Oxford was playing tennis with an
unknown opponent, and probably had a bet on the out-
come of the game. He was swearing as the game pro-
gressed. Philip Sidney, one of the bystanders, objected to
Oxford's swearing. Oxford called Sidney a 'puppy', in
effect telling Sidney to grow up, and probably said that if
he wanted to swear he would swear, as he did not have to
have permission from Sidney to do so. As Sidney was not
playing, only observing, Oxford ejected him from the
court. Sidney must have demanded satisfaction, but
Oxford could not fight a duel as they were not of equal
rank.

In *Twelfth Night* Sir Andrew Aguecheek, who is afraid
to fight a duel with a woman, albeit disguised as a man, is
a caricature of Philip Sidney, later Sir Philip Sidney; and
in Act III, Scene iv, Sir Toby Belch says: "Go to, Sir
Andrew; scout me for him at the corner of the orchard like
a bum-baily: so soon as ever thou seest him, draw; and, as
thou drawst, swear horrible", to which Sir Andrew replies:

"Nay, let me alone for the swearing". This would have been an uproarious line at the court of Elizabeth I in 1580, just after the quarrel on the tennis court that had been caused by Sidney's objections to de Vere's swearing.

While glancing through a book on *King Lear* I came to a passage which said that Shakespeare must have been in a very depressed and despondent state of mind when writing *King Lear* because he had used the word 'nothing' almost forty times. But Shakespeare had used the word 'nothing' almost forty times because the Earl of Oxford was Shakespeare, and his motto was 'Nothing truer than truth'. Oxford had used 'nothing' just as he had used 'true' and 'truth' to identify himself as the author of the plays.

I decided to read *King Lear* to ascertain exactly how and in what context these 'nothings' were used. I immediately found in Act I, Scene i, this famous passage in which Lear says: "Now, our joy, although the last not least . . . . what can you say to draw a third more opulent than your sisters? Speak."

Cordelia:	Nothing my lord.
Lear:	Nothing!
Cordelia:	Nothing.
Lear:	Nothing will come of nothing.

By the time the Earl of Oxford came to write *King Lear* he had sold all of his land and estates: he had nothing. So he used the word 'nothing' as his own personal signature, relating specifically to himself. Everyone at court would have known that his motto was 'Vero nihil verius' meaning 'Truly nothing truer', or 'in truth nothing truer'. Everyone at court would have known that he had nothing. Everyone at court would have known that the Earl of Oxford was 'nothing'. In the same way *Much Ado About Nothing* can be seen as having a second meaning; Much Ado About de Vere.

Seventeen lines after de Vere signs his name in *King Lear*, Lear says: "So young, and so untender?"

Cordelia: So young, my Lord, and true.
Lear: Let it be so; thy truth then be thy dower.

Lear is saying that Cordelia will inherit nothing but her truth. In the space of twenty-four lines de Vere has connected 'nothing' with 'true' and 'truth'; all three words of his motto.

Although the three motto words were fairly close together in *King Lear*, it occurred to me that de Vere may have used them in even closer proximity to each other. When reading the plays I needed to look not only for biographical details, and puns on the characters' names; I should have also to notice how close together were the words 'nothing', 'true', and 'truth'.

Reading the plays had become a voyage of discovery; a thrilling experience. The plays had become new.

In one portrait of the Earl of Oxford he can be seen wearing a pendant shaped like a boar. A blue boar can be seen on the de Vere family crest and, in his more affluent younger days, the Earl of Oxford's yeomen had a blue boar embroidered on their left shoulder. A Latin word for boar is 'verres', which contains the letters 'ver', and therefore, like 'vero' and 'verius', is a pun on the name Ver or Vere. This is why the boar was used as a symbol of the de Vere family. It is also the reason why the boar, and images of the boar, appear so often in the plays and narrative poems of Shakespeare: to reveal that they were written by a de Vere.

While reading *Henry V*, a play in which quite a lot of the action takes place in the Boar's Head Tavern, I began to wonder if any boars are actually blue. In my local library I read about boars in all of the available reference books. Having found nothing, I finally looked in the *Oxford English Dictionary* under 'verres'. Of course there was no entry for 'verres', but there was, and is, an entry for 'verre'. The definition of 'verre', which is from the same French word, is 'a glass', or, 'a vessel made of glass, especially a drinking glass'.

At the time I did not think that this was particularly

significant. Until that is I came to *Henry IV Part Two* (II.iii.21), in which Lady Percy is speaking of Hotspur and says:

> "He was indeed the glass
> Wherein the noble youth did dress themselves.
> He had no legs that practised not his gait;
> And speaking thick, which nature made his blemish,
> Became the accents of the valiant.
> For those that would speak low and tardily
> Would turn their own perfections to abuse
> To seem like him: so that in speech, in gait
> In diet, in affections of delight,
> In military rules, humours of blood,
> He was the mark and glass, copy and book,
> That fashioned others."

The de Vere motto is 'Vero nihil verius', and the de Vere coat of arms shows a 'verres', all puns on the de Vere name, and all frequently found in Shakespeare as 'true', 'truth', 'nothing' and 'boar'. Had de Vere translated the word 'glass' into French and found 'verre', which is also a pun on his name? In this passage, was he really writing about Hotspur, or was he using the word 'glass' to refer to himself?

The entry for Hotspur in the *Dictionary of National Biography* does not say anything at all about his being a leader of fashion in any way whatsoever. It seems that he was interested only in fighting in a succession of battles and wars. The Earl of Oxford, however, was a leader of fashion, particularly after he returned from Italy with his Italian manners and his Italian dress. He had also been the leader of a style of writing, and a manner of speaking: Euphuism.

It therefore seemed to me that de Vere had used the word 'glass' to denote himself and that this passage is indeed about himself and not about Hotspur. But if this is correct, what does 'speaking thick' mean? Apparently, speaking indistinctly, possibly with a foreign accent. Had

all the years of learning French, Latin, Greek, and probably Italian, given de Vere a foreign accent? Did
Shakespeare speak English with a foreign accent? Did the
nobility of England emulate the way he spoke and, if so,
was this the initiation of the English upper class accent?
Although this passage in *Henry IV Part Two* would seem
to indicate that the Earl of Oxford may have spoken with
a foreign accent, it was to be many months before I discovered that this assumption may not necessarily be correct.
I later discovered that the colour blue signifies 'being true'
in heraldry, and therefore the blue boar on the Earl of
Oxford's crest was a true boar and a double-pun on the de
Vere name.

Incidentally, the portrait of the Earl of Oxford, attributed to Marcus Gheeraerts, and the portrait of
Shakespeare, attributed to John Taylor the Younger
(1561-1635), appear to be portraits of the same man, bearing in mind the differences in style of the two portraits,
and also bearing in mind that the portrait of the Earl of
Oxford was painted sometime around 1588 when he was
thirty-eight years old, whereas the portrait of
Shakespeare was painted some twelve to fifteen years
later, when his hair had thinned, and his face had become
fuller and more mature.

In the last scene of *Henry IV Part Two* Pistol tells
Falstaff that: "Thy Doll, and Helen of thy noble thoughts,
is in base durance and contagious prison"; he then says:
"Pistol speaks nought but truth". 'Nought' is an archaic or
poetical word for nothing, and therefore can be translated
into Latin as 'nihil'. 'Truth' has been used instead of 'in
truth', which is part of de Vere's motto, and has been
translated from the Latin 'vero'. So, by using 'nought' and
'truth' in this line de Vere has used two of the three words
of his motto. Finding this partial motto encouraged me to
believe that I might find the whole of it in one of the
plays.

The next play that I read was *Antony and Cleopatra*,
and in Act V, Scene ii, Cleopatra says: "This is my treasurer: let him speak my lord, upon his peril, that I have

reserved to myself nothing. Speak the truth Seleucus". In *Henry IV Part Two* de Vere had used the words 'nought' and 'truth', in *Antony and Cleopatra* he had used 'nothing' and 'truth'; two of the three motto words. Again not all of his motto, but almost.

As well as reading the plays I was also reading the sonnets whenever I could; and while reading sonnet 3, I found these lines:

"Thou art thy mother's glass, and she in thee
Calls back the lovely April of her prime."

In view of the word glass being the French word 'verre', and therefore a pun on the name of Ver or Vere, this line does not only mean 'Thou art the image of thy mother', but also 'Thou art thy mother's verre', 'Thou art thy mother's Vere'. In other words, Edward de Vere is saying 'Thou art my son'.

This pun therefore confirms the Oxfordians' belief that in the sonnets Shakespeare, that is Oxford, was writing to his son. It also confirmed my growing conviction that de Vere had used these puns in every conceivable way, so that his audience and his readers would be constantly aware that he had written the plays and the poems attributed to Shakespeare.

It occurred to me that perhaps de Vere had taken other foreign words that were puns on his name and, after translating them into English, had used them throughout the plays.

Because the Earl of Oxford's motto is in Latin, I decided to start with Cassell's *Latin Dictionary*. There are actually some Latin words that contain the Earl of Oxford's full name: Vere.

The Latin word 'vere' is from the word 'verus', meaning true, just as the 'ver' words in de Vere's motto, 'vero' and 'verius' are also derivations of 'verus', just as when translated into English, truly and truer are derivations of true.

The second Latin word that I noted was 'verecundia',

shame, and 'verecundus', meaning modest, bashful, shy, or having a sense of shame. I already knew that after the words 'true' and 'truth' the word shame is one of the most frequently used words in the whole of Shakespeare; usually indicating the writer's own sense of feeling shame for the way that he had conducted himself during his life.

It occurred to me that Shylock in *The Merchant of Venice* is so called because de Vere had combined the two words shy and lock. Shy is translated from the Latin word 'verecundus', and is therefore a pun on de Vere, whilst lock is Michael Lok, the London merchant.

The next word that I noted was 'veredus', meaning: a swift horse. De Vere mentions horses quite frequently, but did he mean the horse in general, in Latin 'equus', or did he only mean swift horses, hunters?

The final word that I noted was 'vereor', meaning: to be afraid, to fear, to revere, or to have respect for; 'vereri' means: to feel awe, reverence. Again the words fear, and being afraid, are words which are found quite frequently in the works of Shakespeare; but when I saw that 'vereor' means to have respect for, I immediately thought of the passage in *Measure for Measure* where Escalus is questioning Elbow and Pompey:

Elbow: First, an it like you, the house is a respected
            house; next, this is a respected fellow; and
            his mistress is a respected woman.
Pompey: By this hand, sir, his wife is a more respected
            person than any of us all.
Elbow: Varlet, thou liest, thou liest, wicked varlet!
            the time is yet to come that she was ever
            respected with, man, woman, or child.
Pompey: Sir, she was respected with him before he
            married with her.
Escalus: Which is the wiser here? Justice or Iniquity?
            Is this true?
Elbow: O thou caitiff! O thou varlet! O thou wicked
            Hannibal! I respected with her before I mar-
            ried her! If ever I was respected with her, or

she with me, let not your worship think me
the poor Duke's officer.

In this passage Elbow and Pompey use the word respected
instead of suspected, and by so doing, the whole passage
was set up so that de Vere could translate respected into
Latin as being derived from 'vereor': having respect for.
Therefore, each time Elbow and Pompey use the word
respected, the hidden meaning is the Latin word 'vereor',
which is a pun on the name of de Vere. This passage not
only contains respected, Latin 'vereor', but also 'Is this
true?', Latin 'verus', all puns on the name of de Vere; as
well as the 'O' 's, Oxford, and an 'ever', eVer.

I returned to the library and made notes of all of the
Latin words which begin with 'ver', the most important of
which are probably: 'ver', meaning spring; 'verbero',
meaning beat, strike, flog, or whip, all of which happen
frequently throughout the plays of Shakespeare; 'verbero',
meaning someone who deserves to be beaten, flogged, or
whipped, for example a rascal, villain, or a varlet, as
found in the above passage from *Measure for Measure*;
'verbum', a word; 'veritas', truth; 'verna', a slave; 'verto', to
turn, to turn round; 'vertex', the crown of the head, the
summit of a mountain, the pole of the heavens, a gust of
wind, all of which are used throughout Shakespeare
either literally or as a single word abbreviation; for example, crown, head, mountain, heaven.

Edward de Vere had taken these puns on his name,
translated them into English, and then sprinkled them
liberally throughout the plays and poems which we today
attribute to William Shakespeare.

It was not long before the idea came to me that the
Earl of Oxford may have taken these Latin 'ver' words,
puns on his name, and combined them with the Latin
word 'nihil' to create a pun on his Latin motto. He might
then have translated the pun on his motto into English,
and then created a completely new sentence from these
words.

I realized that I would have to read the English words

of the plays, but at the same time I would have to remember which of the English words would, when translated into Latin, be a Latin 'ver' word. These English words would then have to have been combined with the English word 'nothing' (Latin 'nihil') for de Vere to have created a motto pun.

I concluded that the best place to start looking would be *Venus and Adonis*, the first heir of his invention, the first time that he had used the name of William Shakespeare as an author. If the Earl of Oxford had wanted posterity to know that he was Shakespeare then I should find a motto pun in *Venus and Adonis*, but only if he had written *Venus and Adonis*, and only if he were the true author using a motto pun to identify himself.

In *Venus and Adonis*, Adonis tries to escape from the amorous advances of Venus, then:

> "hasteth to his horse.
> But lo, from forth a copse that neighbours by
> A breeding jennet, lusty, young and proud,
> Adonis' trampling courser does espy,
> And forth she rushes, snorts and neighs aloud."

This is followed by an episode in which de Vere contrasts the natural behaviour of the horses with the diffidence of Adonis. The horses "as they were mad, unto the wood they hie them".

This episode is included in the poem so that 'horses' generally, and 'courser' and 'jennet' in particular, can be translated into Latin as 'veredus', and therefore, horse, courser and jennet become puns on the name of de Vere.

Edward de Vere was creating puns, and therefore, as far as he was concerned, 'veredus' was not just a swift horse or hunter, but any horse and every horse. When I came to line 910, I read this:

> "Her more than haste is mated with delays,
> Like the proceedings of a drunken brain,

Full of respects, yet nought at all respecting
In hand with all things, nought at all effecting."

I read it again, "Full of respects, yet nought at all respecting"; respects, nought, respecting; yes, it was a motto pun. The Latin 'vereor' means to have respect for, which had been interpreted by de Vere as simply 'respect'. So the English, respects, nought, respecting, had been translated from the Latin 'vereor', 'nihil', 'vereor', the exact form of de Vere's motto 'vero nihil verius', in which 'vero' and 'verius' are derivations of 'verus'.

Because de Vere was creating puns the Latin derivations of the basic word were irrelevant, and so he had translated the basic Latin 'vereor nihil vereor' as respects nought respecting, because the English derivations of respect were correct for the sentence and the rhyme that he had created in English.

I had found a motto pun. Edward de Vere had written *Venus and Adonis*. This meant that he must have written all of the works of Shakespeare. I was so thrilled and excited that I couldn't stop walking up and down, with everything spinning around in my head.

That night I could not sleep. I was thinking about the motto pun, *Venus and Adonis*, and the episode with the horses. Then it came to me in a flash. The story that Shakspere had been a holder of horses when he first arrived in London was just that: a story. It had been embroidered around a basic horse/veredus pun. Shakspere had not been the holder of horses, he had been the holder of 'veredus'; the holder of 'Vere's'; the holder of Edward de Vere's plays. The story continues that Shakspere had more horses put into his hand than he could hold, and that he had to hire boys to hold the horses for him. Shakspere therefore had a successful horse holding business. This 'horse'/'veredus' pun blows apart the possibility that William Shakspere could have written the plays and poems of William Shakespeare, because it goes straight to the heart of the matter. Shakspere had not been the holder of horses: he had been the holder of de

Vere's plays, and he had become a very successful holder of de Vere's plays.

I decided to read *The Rape of Lucrece* and at line 141 I found:

"The aim of all is but to nurse the life
With honour, wealth and ease, in waning age;
And in this aim there is such thwarting strife
That one for all or all for one we gage."

This seemed to me to be a pun on the Earl of Southampton's motto of: 'Ung par tout, tout par ung'; one for all, all for one. It was not really surprising to find a pun on the Earl of Southampton's motto because *The Rape of Lucrece* like *Venus and Adonis* had been dedicated to the Earl of Southampton.

I did not find a pun on the Earl of Oxford's motto in *The Rape of Lucrece*. Perhaps de Vere had only written the one pun that I had found in *Venus and Adonis*? Perhaps the pun in *Venus and Adonis* had been purely coincidental? Surely not; I was finding too many single word puns on de Vere's name for the motto pun to be co-incidental.

I decided to carry on reading the plays and chose *King John* as the next. I found this line: "Thou wear a lion's hide! doff it for shame and hang a calf's skin on thy recreant limbs'. The Latin word 'versipellis' means to change skin, form, or shape; so, by changing a lion's hide to a calf's skin, the whole of this line was constructed from 'versipellis' and was therefore a 'ver' word and a pun on de Vere's name. The many disguises that take place in the plays of Shakespeare are also a change of form or shape, and are also 'versipellis' and a pun on de Vere's name. This is confirmed by these lines from *Twelfth Night* (I.ii.), Viola says to the Captain: "conceal me what I am, and be my aid for such disguise as haply shall become the form of my intent". A further example of 'versipellis' are these lines from *The Tempest* (I.ii.) where Prospero says to Ariel: "Go make thyself like a nymph o' the sea: be subject to no sight but thine and mine; invisible to every eyeball else. Go take this shape, and hither come in't:".

In Act III, Scene iv, Lewis says: "And bitter shame hath spoiled the sweet world's taste, that it yields nought but shame and bitterness". A pun on de Vere's motto. 'Verecundia', a Latin word meaning a feeling of shame is used instead of 'verus', 'true', to create the pun: 'verecundia, nihil, verecundia'. De Vere had translated this into English as 'shame, nought, shame' and created a new motto or sentence around these words.

Having found two motto puns I now had to discover how many he had written. Were there four or five of these puns waiting to be found somewhere in the thirty-seven plays? Or had he written eight or nine of them? Or had he written a motto pun in every play?

Edward de Vere would have known exactly how many of these puns he had written and, if I were to write a play in which de Vere tells his life story, then I should also have to know exactly how many of these puns he had written.

I found one pun in *A Midsummer Night's Dream* and one pun in *Julius Caesar*; by which time I was expected to find a pun or signature in each of the thirty-seven plays.

However, when I read *Henry V* I found four motto puns, two of them using 'verecundia' as the 'ver' word; one of which, in Act IV, Scene v, is translated as: "Shame, and eternal shame, nothing but shame". The form of this pun: 'verecundia, verecundia, nihil, verecundia', repeating the 'ver' word, then the 'nihil' word, and then the 'ver' word again, was to become a frequently used form of motto pun.

When I read *The Two Gentlemen of Verona* the hidden title of which maybe understood as 'The Two Gentlemen of One de Vere', I came to this passage in Act II, Scene i:

Valentine: No madam; so it stead you, I will write,
          Please you command, a thousand times as much;
          And yet –
Silvia: A pretty period! Well, I guess the sequel;
          And yet I will not name it; – and yet I care not; –

And yet take this again: – and yet I thank you;
Meaning henceforth to trouble you no more.
Speed: *(aside)* And yet you will; and yet another "yet".

When I had first read this passage some months before, I
had thought that Silvia represented Elizabeth I, which of
course she does, and that de Vere was mocking her habit
of using the phrase 'and yet'. However, as I was finding
more and more single word name-puns, as well as motto
puns, I decided to find the entry for 'yet' in the Latin
Dictionary. I found that when 'yet' is used as an adversa-
tive particle, it takes the same translation as 'nevertheless'. The Latin word for 'nevertheless' is 'nihilominus',
which is therefore an alternative word for 'nihil'. In this
passage, and yet, the Latin 'nihilominus', was used to
identify de Vere, just as nothing, the Latin 'nihil', was also
used to identify de Vere.

Finding that 'nihilominus' is an alternative to 'nihil'
meant that de Vere did not have to combine the translation of the 'ver' word with nothing to create a pun on his
motto. He could also combine the translation of the 'ver'
word with and yet, but yet, or simply yet, and this would
also create a motto pun. All de Vere had to do was to write
a line, and then contradict it, as in this passage from
Julius Caesar where Caesar says: "Would he were fatter;
but I fear him not: yet if my name were liable to fear I do
not now the man I should avoid so soon as that spare
Cassius". The contradiction is: "I fear him not: yet if my
name were liable to fear". I fear and to fear were translated from the Latin 'ver' word 'vereri': to fear; and the pun
on the Earl of Oxford's motto is 'vereri, nihilominus,
vereri'.

When creating a motto pun, Oxford uses the word yet
more often than he used the word nothing; and so when I
discovered that 'nihilominus' is an alternative to 'nihil', I
immediately doubled the number of motto puns that I was
finding in the plays.

I was also finding many more 'ver' words: not just
'ver' at the beginning of a word, but also in the middle of a

word and at the end of a word. When a Latin word ends with 'vere', it is because it is the present infinitive active form of a verb. Because de Vere was writing puns, he had in mind the present infinitive form irrespective of tense or person. An example would be the Latin word 'moveo': 'I move'; the present infinitive active form is 'movere': 'to move'. De Vere used 'movere' as the 'ver' word even when he translated it as: 'I move', 'moving' or 'moved'.

In *Julius Caesar* (III.i.), Caesar says: "I could be well moved, if I were as you; if I could pray to move, prayers would move me: but I am constant as the northern star, of whose true fixed and resting quality there is no fellow in the firmament". These lines were constructed from the Latin word 'movere': 'to move'. The northern star is constant and true fixed, and is therefore immovable. Because the northern star is true fixed, and because the word 'true' is a hidden pun on the name of Vere, the star which can be seen on the Earl of Oxford's shield must be the northern star. When Caesar says "I am constant as the northern star", the author is saying that I am Edward de Vere, the Earl of Oxford.

Soon after discovering de Vere's use of the 'ver' words as puns on his name and motto, I also realized that, in English, 'vir' is pronounced the same as 'ver', and that de Vere had used 'vir' words in the same way that he had used 'ver' words.

Some of the most important 'vir' words that de Vere used would be: 'vir', a man, a soldier, especially a foot soldier (and there are many soldiers walking in and out of the plays of Shakespeare, each one of them being a pun on de Vere's name); 'virago', a man-like woman; 'virgo', a maiden, a virgin; 'virgator', one who beats; 'viridarium', a pleasure garden, an orchard (think of all the scenes that take place in a garden or an orchard); 'virtus', virtue, goodness; 'virulentus', full of poison, poisonous, virulent; how many characters are poisoned in the plays of Shakespeare?

Edward de Vere used every word that he could find that would tell his name when pronounced in English.

The Latin word 'via', a street, a road, way, or any passage; 'devius' from 'devia', off the beaten track, out of the way, wandering; 'vehere', to carry, to bear; the Old English words 'vire', fire; 'veir', fair; 'vermeil', from an Old French word meaning blood (think of all the vast amounts of blood that are spilt in the plays of Shakespeare).

As the number of 'ver' words and 'vir' words that I was finding increased day by day, these lines from sonnet 76 became more and more relevant: ". . . . That every word doth almost tell my name . . . . so all my best is dressing old words new . . . .".

This does not mean that one can tell from the style of the writing that it was written by Shakespeare, it means exactly what it says: "every word doth almost tell my name".

To be more precise, every scene in every play, every episode, every twist and turn of the plot was constructed from these hidden puns on de Vere's name. Every major speech, every minor speech, and almost every insignificant speech which today even the most eminent literary academics may not completely understand, was constructed from these hidden puns. In fact almost every single sentence was constructed from at least one of these hidden puns.

For almost four hundred years the Earl of Oxford has been telling us exactly how he constructed the plays that have been attributed to William Shakespeare. In sonnet 76 he wrote: "Why write I still all one, eVer the same, and keep invention in a noted weed, that eVery word doth almost tell my name, showing their birth, and where they did proceed?"; which is followed by ". . . . so all my best is dressing old words new . . . .". The essence of this sonnet is the line: "that every word doth almost tell my name". The Latin word for word is 'verbum', so that every 'verbum' doth almost tell my name; and the name is de Vere, not Shakspere. This conclusion is reinforced when we see that word and name can be connected by the Latin words 'verbis', which is used as meaning in the name of; and 'verbo', in name, in word; as 'verbo' and 'verbis' are both derived from 'verbum'. The Latin phrase 'novare verba' means to invent new words; therefore, de Vere's invention was to dress or interpret old words, the Latin words, in new ways. So these lines, and indeed almost all of the sonnets, were constructed from the Latin word 'verbum'.

There are, on average, about 1400 of these single-word puns on the Earl of Oxford's name in each and every one of the plays that have been attributed to William Shakespeare. Some of the plays contain more than 2000 puns on the name of Vere.

When I found the first motto puns I thought that I might find six or seven in all of the plays. I then revised this by thinking that I might find a pun in each of the thirty-seven plays. As I was searching for puns I was learning something new every day about the words and phrases that de Vere had used and the different ways that he had used them. Consequently, the notes that I was writing for each play were becoming longer and longer, and so I decided to read the first plays again.

After I had read through all of the plays for the first time I had found an average of twelve motto puns. These puns had become too important to be merely a part of a play about the Earl of Oxford's life. Therefore I had to abandon the idea of writing a play and concentrate on writing a book about the puns on the Earl of Oxford's name and motto that can be found in the works of William Shakespeare.

When I came to write the book I read all of the plays again, and this time I found an average of twenty-six motto puns hidden in each and every one of the plays attributed to William Shakespeare. Some of the plays contain more than forty motto puns.

Of the twenty-six pun average, nine were constructed from the Latin 'nihil', and seventeen from 'nihilominus' or other alternatives to 'nihil'. The puns do not always follow the pattern of the Earl of Oxford's motto: 'ver' word, 'nihil' word, 'ver' word. Sometimes the 'nihil' word comes first, occasionally it comes last. Sometimes the 'ver' word may be repeated two or three times. In *The Two Gentlemen of*

Verona (III.ii.) there is a cluster of 'ver' words combined with a cluster of 'nihil' words, spread over six lines and spoken by three characters, as follows:

Proteus: What then?
Valentine: Nothing ('nihil').
Launce: Can nothing ('nihil') speak ('verba facere': to speak)? Master shall I strike ('verberare': to strike)?
Proteus: Who wouldst thou strike ('verberare')?
Launce: Nothing ('nihil').
Proteus: Villain ('verbero') forbear.
Launce: Why sir, I'll strike ('verberare') nothing ('nihil').

These lines were constructed from two definitions of the one Latin word 'verbero', which means one who deserves a flogging, a rascal, a scoundrel, a villain; or, in its verbed form 'verberare' to beat, strike, thrash, or flog. When combined with the repeating of the Latin word 'nihil' this pun on the motto was created: 'nihil, nihil, verberare, verberare, nihil, verbero, verberare, nihil'. These words were translated into English and the dialogue written around them.

In *Julius Caesar* the author did not forget that there were no clocks in 44 B.C. when he wrote the line: "The clock hath stricken three". He wrote the line intentionally, because he knew that the striking of the clock *was* an anachronism, and that the audience at the court of Elizabeth I would recognize it as such. He also realized that the elite audience would know that the Latin word 'verberare' means to strike; and that they would recognize the striking of the clock as being a pun on the name of de Vere.

Ninety per cent of the motto puns are in Latin, the rest are puns in which the 'ver' word is either French, Italian, or Spanish. There are also one or two motto puns in which the 'ver' word is English.

An example of a French 'ver' word pun would be in

Romeo and Juliet (III.ii.) where the Nurse, speaking of Juliet, says to Romeo: "O, she says nothing, sir, but weeps and weeps". Nothing is the Latin word 'nihil', but weeps is the French phrase 'verser des larmes', a pouring of tears; which de Vere dressed or interpreted as 'weeps'. So the pun is 'nihil, verser des larmes, verser des larmes'.

I had to keep an alphabetical notebook of all the various 'ver' words and phrases that Oxford had used in the plays and poems. The last time I counted them there were more than two thousand entries in the notebook. Of course, when de Vere translated these 'ver' words into English they became ordinary English words that anyone and everyone could use. However, it is the way that these words were used in the works of Shakespeare which identifies the Earl of Oxford as being the author. Other writers used the same words, but not in the same way.

First of all de Vere used these 'ver' words in the titles of plays, *The Two Gentlemen of Verona* and *Much Ado About Nothing* have already been mentioned. Other plays are: *Measure for Measure*, the French word 'verre' is a measure of a jug, glass, or pot, the Latin phrase 'vertere modum' is a measure in music, and the Old English word 'verge' is a measure in carpentry; *A Midsummer Night's Dream*, the Spanish 'verano' means summer, and the French 'rever' means to dream; *Love's Labour's Lost*, the Latin 'sulcos in pulvere ducere' means to draw or make a furrow in the dust, which is transferred as meaning to labour in vain. *All's Well that Ends Well* and *The Comedy of Errors* are also titles that were created from puns on de Vere's name.

The title *As You Like It* is absolutely meaningless and has no relevance whatsoever to the plot of the play. So why did Shakespeare choose this title? He chose it because the French phrase 'comme tu veux' not only means 'as you like' but also because it sounds very much like Comte de Ver, meaning Count or Earl de Ver, who could be none other than Edward de Vere, Earl of Oxford. 'Comme tu veux' can also be interpreted as meaning 'what you will', and *What You Will* is the sub-title of *Twelfth*

Night. The equally meaningless title of *The Winter's Tale* was presumably created because in French it becomes *Le Conte d'Hiver*, a witty pun on 'Le Comte de Ver'.

De Vere used 'ver' words when setting the scene, and also in stage directions. An example would be the famous direction in *Cymbeline* (V.v.): "Jupiter descends in thunder and lightning, sitting upon an eagle. He throws a thunderbolt. The ghosts fall on their knees".

"Jupiter descends" was constructed from the Latin word 'provolvere' meaning to descend, to lower oneself; "sitting on an eagle" from 'aviarius', relating to birds; "The ghosts" was constructed from 'simulacra virtutis', an appearance, apparition, phantom; and "fall on their knees" from 'se advolvere', to throw oneself at the feet of, of supplicants.

Sometimes de Vere used the English translation of the 'ver' word in such a way that it explains the meaning of the Latin word. One of the best examples of this is the line from *King John* which explains the meaning of the Latin 'versipellis', as noted earlier.

Another example is from *Antony and Cleopatra* (IV.xv.), where Antony says: "Now my spirit is going; I can no more". To which Cleopatra says: "Noblest of men, woo't die?" And as Antony dies she says: "O, see, my women, the crown o' the earth doth melt". The Latin words 'dissolvere animam' mean to dissolve the spirit; but as 'dissolvere' can also mean to melt, 'dissolvere animam' can also mean to melt the spirit; this passage was therefore constructed from 'dissolvere animam'. Towards the end of the play Charmian says: "Dissolve ('dissolvere'), thick cloud, and rain, that I may say the gods do weep". Cleopatra then says to the asp: "Come, thou mortal wretch, with thy sharp teeth this knot intrinsicate untie". The Latin 'dissolvere' can also mean to untie; and therefore de Vere also constructed this passage from 'dissolvere animam', which he interpreted as to untie life. Because 'dissolvere animam' means to dissolve, melt, untie, or release the spirit, it can be transferred as meaning to die.

It is the way that de Vere grouped the 'ver' words in

clusters that helps to identify him as being Shakespeare. The repetition of respected, from the Latin word 'vereor', in *Measure for Measure* is an example of the way de Vere clustered a single 'ver' word; as is the word strike, Latin 'verbero' in *The Two Gentlemen of Verona*.

Another example also comes from *The Two Gentlemen of Verona* (I.i.):

Speed: Twenty to one, then, he is shipped already
            And I have played the sheep in losing him.
Proteus: Indeed, a sheep doth very often stray
            An if the shepherd be awhile away.
Speed: You conclude that my master is a shepherd
            then, and I a sheep.
Proteus: I do.
Speed: Why then, my horns are his horns, whether I
            wake or sleep.
Proteus: A silly answer and fitting well a sheep.
Speed: This proves me still a sheep.
Proteus: True; and thy master a shepherd.
Speed: Nay, that I can deny by a circumstance.
Proteus: It shall go hard but I'll prove it by another.
Speed: The shepherd seeks the sheep, and not the
            sheep the shepherd; but I seek my master,
            and my master seeks not me; therefore I am
            no sheep.
Proteus: The sheep for fodder follow the shepherd; the
            shepherd for food follows not the sheep: thou
            for thy wages followest thy master; thy mas-
            ter for wages follows not thee: therefore thou
            art a sheep.

The latin word 'vervex' means a sheep, a dolt, and was used as a term of abuse. The 7th edition (1967) of Cassell's *Italian-English Dictionary* says that the word 'vergaro' is a shepherd. So 'vervex' and 'vergaro' are 'ver' words and are puns on de Vere's name. For those in the Elizabethan theatres who could understand the hidden wit in the plays of Shakespeare, this passage would have been an additional source of humour, completely lost to us today.

Another form of clustering that de Vere uses is to take one 'ver' word and translate it into more than one English word, as in the passage from *The Two Gentlemen of Verona* where the Latin word 'verbero' is translated as strike and villain.

A typical example of this can be found in the opening lines of *Macbeth*:

First Witch: When shall we three meet ('obviam', to meet in a friendly or hostile manner) again?
                In thunder, lightning, or in rain ('pluvia')?
Second Witch: When the hurlyburly's ('obviam ire', to confront) done,
                when the battle's ('obviam ire') lost and won.
First Witch: Where the place?
Second Witch: Upon the heath ('invia': a trackless place).
Third Witch: There to meet ('obviam') with Macbeth.

When the First Witch asks 'Where the place?', it gave de Vere the opportunity to use the Latin word 'invia': a trackless place; which he interpreted as 'Upon the heath'. De Vere must also have interpreted 'obviam ire', to confront as 'hurlyburly', and 'battle', because firstly 'obviam ire' connects with 'obviam', to meet; and secondly because he actually used the word 'confronted' in scene ii. These lines were therefore created from the Latin words 'obviam', 'obviam ire', 'pluvia', and 'invia', all of which are derived from 'via', pronounced 'Vere'.

A further example is the Latin word 'intervertere', meaning to intercept; but which can be transferred as meaning to embezzle, to rob. De Vere extends this to mean to rob, to steal, to filch, to cheat, to pocket, etc.

In *Othello* (III.iii.), Iago says:

"Who steals my purse steals trash; 'tis something, nothing;

'Twas mine, 'tis his, and has been slave to thousands, but he that filches from me my good name robs me of that which not enriches him and makes me poor indeed."

This passage has been created around the Latin word 'intervertere', which de Vere used four times, translated as: steals, steals, filches, and robs. As these words have also been combined with nothing, Latin 'nihil', the passage is also a motto pun: 'intervertere, intervertere, nihil, intervertere, intervertere'. The emphatic use of the Latin word 'vere' can mean indeed, and therefore the hidden meaning of "he that filches from me my good name robs me of that which not enriches him and makes me poor indeed" is 'and makes me poor Vere'; and of course, when compared to what he had been, de Vere was poor after he had sold his lands and estates.

Incidentally, the whole of the central dialogue between Othello and Iago in this scene was constructed from the Latin 'advertere' meaning: to turn towards (of thoughts); 'verso', to think over, which de Vere interpreted as simply 'think'; 'veritas', truth, which is transferred as honesty; 'verus', truthful, which de Vere interpreted as honest from 'veritas', honesty; and the emphatic use of the Latin 'vere', indeed. Furthermore, the Latin word 'diverbium' means a dialogue on the stage; so that every word of the dialogue is a pun on de Vere's name.

An interesting example of how de Vere clustered 'ver' words, and then extended the translation in every possible way can be found in *Macbeth* (IV.iv.):

First Witch: Round about the cauldren go
             In the poison'd entrails throw.
             Toad, that under cold stone
             Days and nights has thirty one
             Swelter'd venom sleeping got,
             Boil thou first i' the charmed pot.
All: Double, double toil and trouble;
             fire burn and cauldren bubble.

Second Witch: Fillet of a fenny snake,
In the cauldren boil and bake;
Eye of newt and toe of frog,
Wool of bat and tongue of dog,
Adder's fork and blind worm's sting,
Lizard's leg and howlet's wing,
For a charm of powerful trouble
Like a hell-broth boil and bubble.
All: Double, double toil and trouble;
Fire burn and cauldren bubble.   etc.

It is supposed that Shakespeare obtained the recipe of this witch's broth from a real witch, and that when it is recited it brings bad luck to the production of the play. This is the origin of the superstitions that surround the 'Scottish play'. The witch from whom Shakespeare obtained the recipe was an Italian witch, as the 7th edition (1967) of Cassell's *Italian-English Dictionary* says that 'versiera' means a witch, a she devil. 'Versiera' is a pun on de Vere's name, so de Vere was the witch who supplied the recipe. All of the ingredients in the gruel are either: appertaining to snakes, which de Vere has extended to include reptiles and reptile-like creatures; or poisons, which de Vere has extended to include poisonous animals and animals that may be thought of as being poisonous or malignant. All of the ingredients are boiled in the cauldron that is bubbling on the burning fire.

The Latin word 'fervere' means to boil, and a definition of the English word virulent in the *Oxford English Dictionary* is: of serpents, material substances, plants etc., possessing venomous or strongly poisonous qualities; which is from the Latin 'virulentus' meaning poison, poisonous, virulent. Therefore, the whole of this witch's brew was created from the Latin words 'fervere' and 'virulentus', both name puns.

Most of the lines of the Chorus in *Henry V* were constructed from the same Latin words found in the middle section of *Othello* (III.iii.); 'advertere' to turn thoughts;

'animadvertere' to turn over in the mind; and 'versare' to think over. As for example the Prologue to Act I: "Piece out our imperfections with your thoughts ('advertere') .... think ('verso'), when we talk of horses, that you see them printing their proud hooves i' th' receiving earth: for 'tis your thoughts ('advertere') that now must deck our kings. Carry them here and there: jumping o'er times; turning ('convertere' to turn, to change; which connects with 'advertere') th' accomplishment of many years into an hour glass ....". In the Prologue to Act III: "Thus with imagined wing our swift scene flies, in motion of no less celerity than that of thought ('advertere') .... O, do but think ('verso') you stand upon the rivage, and behold a city on th' inconstant billows dancing .... Follow, follow! Grapple your minds ('animadvertere') to sternage ('advertere' of ships, to steer) of this navy .... Work, work your thoughts ('advertere'), and therein see a siege .... Still be kind, and eke out our performance with your mind ('animadvertere'). In the Prologue to Act V: "Now we bear the king toward Calais: grant him there; there seen, heave him away upon your winged thoughts ('advertere'), athwart the sea .... So swift a pace hath thought ('advertere'), that even now you may imagine him upon Blackheath .... But now behold, in the quick forge and working house of thought ('advertere'), how London doth pour out her citizens .... Now in London place him ... and omit all the occurrences, whatever chanced, till Harry's back returned ('revertor' to turn back; which connects with 'advertere') again to France .... Then brook abridgement, and your eyes advance, after your thoughts ('advertere'), straight back again to France". And in the Epilogue the Chorus begins: "Thus far, with rough and all-unable pen, our bending ('versare', to bend, to turn, to turn over in the mind, to think over) author hath pursued the story ...".

In the closing lines of *Henry VI Part Three*, Gloucester says: "Indeed (Latin 'vere'), 'tis true ('verus') that Henry told me of; for I have often heard my other say I came into the world with my legs forward .... Then, since the heavens have shaped my body (the Latin 'perversus' means deformed), let hell make crooked ('perversus' also means crooked) my mind to answer it . . . .". This theme is continued in Gloucester's opening speech in *Richard III*: "But I, that am not shaped for sportive tricks ('perversus', deformed) . . . I, that am rudely stamped ('perversus', deformed) . . . I, that am curtailed of this fair proportion, cheated of feature by dissembling Nature, deformed ('perversus'), unfinished ('perversus'), sent before my time into this breathing world, scarce half made up ('perversus') . . . why, I . . . have no delight to pass away the time, unless to spy my shadow in the sun and descant on mine own deformity ('perversus'): and therefore . . . I am determined to prove the villain and hate the idle pleasures of these days".

In Scene ii Anne says to Gloucester: "Blush, blush, thou lump of foul deformity ('perversus')"; but then de Vere begins to use a second definition of 'perversus' when Anne says: "God grant me too thou may'st be damned for that wicked ('perversus' also means wicked) deed". In Gloucester's soliloquy he returns to the first definition: "and will she yet abase her eyes on me . . . on me, that halts and am misshaped ('perversus') thus?". In Scene iii Gloucester says: "I am too childish-foolish for this world"; to which Queen Margaret replies: "Hie thee to hell for shame and leave this world, thou cacodemon!". The Latin 'avernus' means the infernal regions; which I believe de Vere interpreted as hell, and a cacodemon was an evil spirit and is therefore derived from 'perversus', which in this instance means evil.

In Scene iii, line 306 we find these lines:

Gloucester: I cannot blame her: by God's holy mother, she hath had too much wrong; and I repent my part thereof that I have done to her.

Queen Elizabeth: I never did her any, to my knowledge.

Gloucester: Yet you have all the vantage of her wrong.

The Latin word 'perversus' can also mean wrong or wrongdoing, so these lines were constructed from 'perversus'. Queen Elizabeth's line was inserted by de Vere so that he could have Gloucester say "Yet", which is the Latin 'nihilominus'. Therefore, when 'perversus' was combined with 'nihilominus' de Vere created this motto pun: 'perversus, nihilominus, perversus'.

De Vere returned to the deformed definition of 'perversus' in Act IV, Scene iv with the lines he gave to Queen Elizabeth: "O, thou didst prophesy the time would come that I should wish for thee to help me curse that bottled spider, that foul bunch backed ('perversus') toad.". In addition to 'perversus' other words in these lines that are name puns include: 'veridici cantus', a prophecy; 'avere', to wish; 'servire' or 'adiuvare', to help; 'devovere', to curse; and 'virulentus', venomous, poisonous; which was interpreted by de Vere as spider and toad.

At line 368 there begins a long passage that was constructed from 'perversus' and the Latin phrase 'verbis conceptis iurare', which means to take an oath according to the usual form, to swear:

King Richard: I swear ('verbis conceptis iurare').
Queen Elizabeth: By nothing ('nihil'); for this is no oath ('verbis conceptis iurare') . . . if something ('non nihil') thou wouldst swear ('verbis conceptis iurare') to be believed, swear ('verbis conceptis iurare') then by something ('non nihil') that thou hath not wronged ('perversus' wrong doing).
King Richard: Now, by the world-
Queen Elizabeth: 'Tis full of thy foul wrongs ('perversus').
King Richard: Why then, by God-
Queen Elizabeth: God's wrong ('perversus') is most of all. If thou didst fear ('vereri', to fear) to break an oath ('verbis conceptis iurare') with Him . . . . If thou didst fear ('vereri') to break an oath ('verbis con-

	ceptis iurare') by Him . . . What canst thou swear ('verbis conceptis iurare') by now?
King Richard:	The time to come.
Queen Elizabeth:	That thou has wronged ('perversus') in the time o'erpast; for I myself have many tears to wash hereafter time, for time past wronged ('perversus') by thee.

Although I have not included every line in this extract, the whole of this passage becomes a triple motto pun when the repeating of 'perversus', 'verbis conceptis iurare', and 'vereri' are combined with 'nihil' and the repeated 'non nihil', nothing and something.

In Act V, Scene i, Buckingham recognizes his own complicity in the wrongdoings of Richard with these lines: "This, this All Souls' day to my fearful soul is the determined respite of my wrongs ('perversus') . . . Come, lead me, officers, to the block of shame ('verecundia'); wrong ('perversus') hath but wrong ('perversus'), and blame the due of blame.

The appearance of the ghosts in Scene iii was suggested by the Latin phrase 'simulacra virtutis', meaning an appearance, an apparition, a phantom; and the reason for the appearance of the ghosts is to turn the wrongdoings of Richard back onto himself. The ghost of Prince Edward says to Richmond: "Be cheerful, Richmond; for the wronged ('perversus') souls of butchered princes fight in thy behalf". The ghost of Clarence says to Richmond: "Thou offspring of the house of Lancaster, the wronged ('perversus') heirs of York do pray for the". And the ghost of Vaughan says to Richmond: "Awake, and think ('versare') our wrongs ('perversus') in Richard's bosom will conquer him!". In this line 'perversus' was connected to 'pervertere', meaning to overthrow; which was interpreted by de Vere as being to 'conquer'; so that Richard's wrongs will wrong him.

It can therefore be seen that the hidden Latin word

'perversus' meaning bad, evil, wrong, wrongdoing, as well as deformed and crooked, is one of the predominant words of *Richard III*, and that the influence of this word can be felt throughout the whole of the play.

The opening lines of *Hamlet* show that de Vere did indeed interpret the Latin phrase 'simulacra virtutis' as meaning a ghost, as follows:

Marcellus: What, has this thing appear'd ('simulacra virtutis', an appearance) again tonight?

Bernardo: I have seen nothing ('nihil').

Marcellus: Horatio says 'tis but our fantasy, and will not let belief take hold of him touching this dreaded sight, twice seen of us; therefore I have entreated him along with us to watch the minutes of this night, that if again this apparition ('simulacra virtutis', an apparition) come, he may approve our eyes and speak ('verba facit emortuo', he talks to the dead) to it.

Horatio: Tush, tush, 'twill not appear ('simulacra virtutis', an appearance).

Cassell's *Latin Dictionary* (1987) says that 'simulacrum' can be transferred as meaning a shade or ghost of the dead, and that 'simulacra virtutis' means a phantom, appearance; an earlier edition also added an apparition. In these lines de Vere used two definitions of 'simulacra virtutis', an appearance, and an apparition, in relation to the ghost; therefore he must have interpreted the third definition, a phantom, as being a ghost. It is another example of how he used the literal translation of a Latin word or phrase, as well as his own interpretation of the word or phrase, within the context of the dialogue.

The predominant hidden words in the scenes in *A Midsummer Night's Dream* that involve the four lovers Lysander, Demetrius, Hermia, and Helena are 'subducere viatica', meaning to steal away; 'persequi omnis vias', meaning to follow, to pursue, to use every method or way;

and 'de via decedere', meaning to depart from one's course, to go astray; which was interpreted by de Vere as 'lost'. Each of these phrases is derived from the Latin word 'via': a way, highway, street, course, journey, method. However, probably the most interesting lines in the play are those that are spoken by Lysander in Act III, Scene ii: "Ay ('vero'), by my life! And never did desire ('avere' to desire) to see (Spanish 'ver' to see) thee more. Therefore be out of hope, of question or doubt: be certain: nothing ('nihil') truer ('verius'): 'tis no jest that I do hate thee and love Helena". The words "nothing truer", which are translated from the Latin 'nihil verius', are the second and third words of Oxford's motto. the word 'vero', the first word of the motto, can mean: to be sure, certainly; but instead of interpreting 'vero' as meaning: to be sure, certainly; it would seem that de Vere interpreted it as meaning: be certain; and by so doing, the hidden meaning of 'be certain: nothing truer' is 'vero nihil verius' which is his exact motto. The 'vero' of the motto then connects with the 'vero' at the beginning of these lines which was translated as 'Ay'. The Latin word 'controversia' means a lawsuit; and is transferred as meaning: dispute, doubt, and question; which is the definition that was intended by de Vere. Therefore, these lines were constructed from the Latin 'vero, controversia, controversia, vero, nihil, verius', which is a hidden motto pun containing the actual motto.

The combination of the puns on his motto, and the different ways in which he utilized the single word puns on his name, are a unique way of recognizing the plays and poems of the Earl of Oxford.

Probably the most common form of motto pun is when two or more 'ver' words are repeated and combined with 'nihil' or 'nihilominus', which may also have been repeated, to create a multiple word motto pun. An example of this type of motto pun can be found in the 'verbis conceptis iurare', 'perversus', 'vereri' episode of *Richard III*.

Another example of one of these complex puns on the Earl of Oxford's motto can be found in Cranmer's speech in the last scene of *Henry VIII*:

King: I thank ye (Latin 'grates persolvere' to
          express thanks) heartily; so shall this lady,
          when she has so much English.
Cranmer: Let me speak (Latin 'verba facere'), sir . . . .
          and the words ('verba') I utter ('verba facere')
          let none think flattery, for they'll find 'em
          truth ('veritas'). This royal infant – heaven
          still (Latin 'nihilominus') move ('movere')
          about her! – though in her cradle, yet
          ('nihilominus') now promises ('fidem solvere')
          upon this land a thousand thousand bless-
          ings (Latin 'veridici cantus' a prophecy). She
          shall be – a pattern to all princes living with
          her and all that shall succeed ('veridici can-
          tus') . . . . All princely graces that mould up
          such a mighty ('viripotens') piece as this is,
          with all the Virtues ('virtus') that attend the
          good ('virtuosus'), shall still ('nihilominus') be
          doubled on her ('veridici cantus').
          Truth ('veritas') shall nurse ('fovere') her
          ('veridici cantus') . . . . she shall be loved
          and feared ('vereri' to fear) . . . . her foes
          ('adversarii') shake ('commovere' to shake)
          like a field of beaten corn, and hang their
          heads with sorrow ('veridici cantus'). Good
          ('virtuosus') grows with her ('veridici cantus')
          . . . . and those about her from her shall
          read the perfect ways of honour ('verum')
          . . . . Nor shall this peace sleep with her;
          but as when the bird of wonder ('admira-
          tionem movere' to astonish, surprise) dies
          ('dissolvere animam'), the maiden ('virgini-
          tas') phoenix, her ashes new create another
          heir as great in admiration ('admirationem
          movere') as herself ('veridici cantus'). So shall
          she leave her blessedness to one . . . . who
          from the sacred ashes of her honour ('verum')
          shall star like rise, as great in fame as she
          was ('veridici cantus') . . . . WhereVer the

	bright sun of heaven shall shine, his honour ('verum') and the greatness of his name shall be, and make new nations ('veridici cantus').
King:	Thou speakest wonders ('admirationem movere' to move to wonder, admiration, surprise, astonishment).
Cranmer:	She shall be, to the happiness of England, an aged princess; many days shall see her, and yet ('nihilominus') no day without a deed to crown it ('veridici cantus') . . . . but she must die ('dissolvere animam'), she must, the saints must have her; yet ('nihilominus') a virgin ('virginitas'), a most unspotted lily shall she pass to th' ground, and all the world ('universitas') shall mourn ('veridici cantus').

The whole of Cranmer's speech was constructed from 'veridici cantus' a prophecy; but it also includes the repeating of 'verba', 'virtus', 'virtuosus', 'verum', 'virginitas', 'admirationem movere' with 'movere' and 'commovere', and 'dissolvere animam' with 'grates persolvere' and 'fidem solvere'; therefore, with the repeating of 'nihilominus' nevertheless, in the form of yet and still, the whole speech is a multiple word motto pun.

One of the most predominant hidden words in *Henry VIII* is the Latin word 'verus', true; together with its derivations including, as in this episode 'verum' honour. Perhaps this is the reason why the alternative title of the play is *All Is True*, which was the title by which the play was originally known. The hidden meaning of the title *All Is True* would therefore be All Is de Vere, which could be interpreted as meaning that all of the play was written by de Vere.

Another example of a multiple word motto pun can be found in *Much Ado About Nothing* (II.i.):

Don Pedro:	Now, Signior, where's the Count? Did you see him?

Benedick:	I told him, and I think I told him true ('vere'), that your grace had got the good will of this young lady; and I offered him my company to a willow tree, either to make him a garland ('virgatus', made of twigs or osiers), as being forsaken, or to bind him up a rod ('virga'), as being worthy to be whipped ('verbero', deserving to be whipped).
Don Pedro:	To be whipped ('verberare')! What's his fault?
Benedick:	The flat transgression of a school boy, who, being oVerjoyed with finding a bird's nest ('aviarius', relating to birds), shows it his companion, and he steals ('avertere', to steal; or 'intervertere', to purloin) it.
Don Pedro:	Wilt thou make a trust a transgression? The transgression is in the stealer ('aversor').
Benedick:	Yet ('nihilominus') it had not been amiss the rod ('virga') had been made, and the garland ('virgatus') too, for the garland ('virgatus') he might have worn himself, and the rod ('virga') he might have bestowed on you, who, as I take it, have stolen ('avertere' or 'intervertere') his bird's nest ('aviarius', relating to birds).
Don Pedro:	I will but teach them to sing ('cantare convivia', to sing of), and restore them to the owner.
Benedick:	If their singing ('cantare convivia') answer your saying, by my faith, you say honestly.

Both the garland and the rod would be made from the osiers of the willow tree and would therefore be the Latin words 'virgatus', made of twigs or osiers; and 'virga', a rod for beating. An alternative word for the garland could be 'verbenatus': crowned with sacred boughs. The line "as being worthy to be whipped" was used by de Vere because the Latin word 'verbero' means deserving to be whipped; and it is another example of how he used the literal translation of a Latin word in his dialogue. This episode was constructed from 'virga', 'virgatus' or 'verbenatus', 'verbero', 'aviarius', 'avertere' or 'intervertere', and 'cantare convivia'; all of which were repeated and combined with 'nihilominus' to create a multiple word motto pun.

The Latin word 'veritas' means truth, the nature of things; but the *Latin Dictionary* (1879) by Lewis and Short gives a second definition, which is: Nature, the truth of nature. A third usage is as 'imitari veritatem' which Cassell's *Latin Dictionary* translates as: to be true to nature, of works of art. It can therefore be seen from *The Winter's Tale* (IV.iv.) that de Vere connected 'veritas', which he interpreted as meaning simply nature, with 'imitari veritatem', which he interpreted as meaning simply art, as follows:

Perdita: [to Polixenes] Sir, welcome ('salvere iubere', to welcome to one's home) . . . . [to Camillo] You're welcome ('salvere iubere'), sir. Give me those flowers there Dorcas. ReVerend sirs. For you there's rosemary and rue; these keep seeming and saVour all the winter (French 'hiver' or Italian 'inverno') long. Grace ('favor') and rememberance be to you both, and welcome ('salvere iubere') to our shearing (Latin 'oviarius', of or belonging to sheep).

Polixenes: Shepherdess, a fair (Old English 'veir') one are you, well you fit our ages with flowers of winter (French 'hiver' or Italian 'inverno').

Perdita: Sir, the year growing ancient, not yet on summer's (Spanish 'verano') death, nor on the birth of trembling winter (Italian 'inverno'), the fairest flowers o' the season are our carnations and streak'd gillyVors, which some call nature's (Latin 'veritas', nature) bastards: of that kind our rustic garden's (Latin 'viridarium', a pleasure garden) barren; and I care not to get slips of them.

Polixenes: Wherefore, gentle maiden (Latin 'virgo'), do you neglect them.

Perdita:	For I have heard it said there is an art (Latin 'imitari veritatem', of works of art, to be true to nature) which in their piedness (Latin 'versicolor', changing colour, of various colours, parti-coloured) shares with great creating nature ('veritas').
Polixenes:	Say there be; yet ('nihilominus') nature ('veritas') is made better by no mean (Latin 'via', method, way or mean), but nature ('veritas') makes that mean ('via'): so, oVer that art ('imitari veritatem') which you say adds to nature ('veritas'), is an art ('imitari veritatem') that nature ('veritas') makes. You see, sweet maid ('virgo'), we marry a gentler scion to the wildest stock, and make conceive a bark of baser kind by bud of nobler race: this is an art ('imitari veritatem') which does mend nature ('veritas'), change (Latin 'convertere', to change) it rather, but the art ('imitari veritatem') itself is nature ('veritas').
Perdita:	So it is ('vere', indeed).
Polixenes:	Then make your garden ('viridarium') gillyVors, and do not call them bastards.
Perdita:	I'll not put the dibble in earth to set one slip of them; no more than were I painted I would wish (Latin 'avere', to wish) this youth should say 'twere well, and only therefore desire ('avere', to desire) to breed by me ('imitari veritatem', the likeness of life in works of art).

The Latin word 'nothus' means bastard, and because 'nothus' sounds like nothing it is possible that de Vere intended 'bastard' to be a substitute for nothing when he was creating motto puns. In this episode de Vere calls the grafting of plants an "art" because the Latin 'imitari veritatem' means to be true to nature, of works of art; or literally to copy or imitate nature, which connects with his interpretation of 'veritas' as being nature. De Vere constructs Perdita's closing lines from an interpretation of 'imitari veritatem' that means the likeness of life in works of art. Therefore this episode was constructed from 'imitari veritatem' and 'veritas' as well as 'salvere iubere', 'via', 'viridarium', 'hiver' or 'inverno' with 'verano', 'versicolor' with 'convertere', 'virgo', 'gillyvors', and 'avere'; which, when combined with 'nihilominus' and the repeated 'nothus', created a multiple word motto pun.

If anyone were to suggest that puns like these are merely coincidental, then they will have to find the same amount of coincidence in every single play written during the Elizabethan and Jacobean periods. The difficulty that they will face in their search for this level of coincidence is that it just is not there to be found; therefore, those plays that contain a large number of motto puns, many of them in these quite complex forms, must have been written by the Earl of Oxford.

Edward de Vere constructed his plays in episodes, each being constructed from a framework of two or more 'ver' words, each of which was repeated two or more times. These episodes were then connected to each other to form the scenes. It is possible to follow the sense of an episode by reading only those lines which contain 'ver' words and phrases, as in this episode from *Much Ado About Nothing*, which is actually the whole of Act IV, Scene ii:

Verges:	We have the exhibition to examine ('veri' or 'verum investigare').
Sexton:	. . . which are the offenders that are to be examined (Latin 'veri inquisitio atque investigatio', a searching into, an examination)? Let them come before Master Constable (Old English 'verderer', a petty constable of a city ward, now obsolete, *OED*).
Dogberry:	What is your name, friend (Latin 'amicus verus')?
Borachio:	Borachio.
Dogberry:	Pray write down (Italian 'mettere a verbale',

to set down in writing: or 'scrivere a verbale',
to include in the record) 'Borachio' . . . .
Yours, sirrah?

Conrade: I am a gentleman, sir, and my name is
Conrade.

Dogberry: Write down ('mettere a verbale') 'Master
Gentleman Conrade' . . . Masters, do you
serve (Latin 'servire' to serve) God?

Conrade and
Borachio: Yea ('vero'), sir, we do.

Dogberry: Write down ('mettere a verbale') that they
hope they serve ('servire') God: and write
(Italian 'scrivere', to write) God first, for God
defend but God should go before such villains
(Latin 'verberones') . . . . . . Masters, it is
proved already that you are little better than
false knaves, and it will go near to be
thought (Latin 'advertere', of thought, to turn
toward) so shortly.

Conrade: Marry, sir, we say we are none.

Dogberry: Come you hither sirrah: a word ('verbum') in
your ear. Sir, I say to you, it is thought
('advertere') you are false knaves.

Borachio: Say, I say to you, we are none.

Dogberry: Have you writ down ('mettere a verbale'),
that they are none?

Sexton: Master Constable ('verderer'), you go not the
way (Latin 'via', a way, method) to examine
('verum investigare'). You must call forth the
watch that are their accusers.

Dogberry: Yea ('vero'), marry, that's the eftest way
('via'), let the watch come forth. Masters, I
charge you in the prince's name (Latin 'regulus verbis', in the name of the prince) accuse
these men ('viri').

First Watchman: This man ('vir') said, sir, that Don John
the prince's brother was a villain ('verbero').

Dogberry: Write down ('mettere a verbale') 'Prince John
a villain ('verbero')' . . . Why this is flat per-

jury ('verbis conceptis periurare'), to call a prince's brother a villain ('verbero').

Borachio: Master Constable ('verderer')–

Sexton: What heard you him say else?

Second Watchman: Marry, that he had received a thousand ducats of Don John, for accusing the Lady Hero wrongfully ('perversus', wrong doing).

First Watchman: And that Count Claudio did mean, upon his words ('verba'), to disgrace Hero before the whole assembly, and not marry her.

Dogberry: O villain ('verbero')!

Sexton: And this is more, masters, than you can deny ('infitior verum', to deny). Prince John is this morning secretly stolen away ('subducere viatica', to steal away): Hero was in this manner ('via', manner) accused, in this very ('verus') manner ('via') refused, and upon the grief of this suddenly died. Master Constable ('verderer'), let these men ('viri') be bound, and brought to Leonato's, I will go before and show him their examination ('veri inquisitio atque investigatio').   [exit]

Dogberry: Come, let them be opinioned ('animadversio' a punishment; or 'verberatio' also a punishment, which would connect with 'verbero').

Conrade: Off, coxcomb!

Dogberry: God's my life, where's the sexton? Let him write down ('mettere a verbale') the prince's officer 'coxcomb' . . .

Conrade: Away (Italian 'via')! you are an ass, you are an ass.

Dogberry: O that he were here to write me down ('mettere a verbale') an ass! but, masters, remember that I am an ass – though it be not written down ('mettere a verbale'), yet ('nihilominus') forget not that I am an ass. No, villain ('verbero'), thou art full of piety . . . .

Bring him away (Italian 'via'). O that I had
been writ down ('mettere a verbale') an ass!

The phrase that dominates this scene is the Italian 'mettere a verbale', but other 'ver' words and phrases that are
repeated are 'veri inquisitio atque investigatio' with 'veri'
or 'verum investigare' and 'infitior verum', 'verbero',
'advertere', 'regulus verbis' with 'verbis conceptis periurare', 'subducere viatica' with 'via', meaning both way and
manner, which was also combined with the Italian 'via',
and the Old English 'verderer'. The scene concludes with
a 'nihilominus' and therefore Dogberry's closing lines contain a motto pun 'mettere a verbale, nihilominus, mettere
a verbale', although the whole scene could be interpreted
as being a multiple-word motto pun.

One of the most witty puns on the motto in all of the
works of Shakespeare can be found in these lines from
Twelfth Night (IV.ii.):

Feste: What is the opinion of Pythagoras concerning
            wild fowl (Latin 'aviarius', the haunt of wild
            birds in the woods; or, relating to birds)?
Malvolio: That the soul of our grandam (Latin 'avia')
            might haply inhabit a bird ('aviarius', relat-
            ing to birds).
Feste: What thinkest (Latin 'versare', to think over)
            thou of his opinion?
Malvolio: I think (Latin 'verso') nobly of the soul, and
            no way ('via') approve his opinion.
Feste: Fare thee well (Latin 'avere'): remain thou
            still ('nihilominus' nevertheless) in darkness.
            Thou shalt hold the opinion of Pythagoras ere
            I will allow of thy wits, and fear to kill a wood-
            cock ('aviarius') lest thou dispossess the soul of
            thy grandam ('avia'). Fare thee well ('avere').

On the surface these lines are just silly nonsense and are
usually omitted from most productions, (including Trevor
Nunn's recent film, 1996) but underneath they contain

one of the most witty and brilliant puns on his motto that Oxford ever wrote. The Latin word 'avia', a grandmother, is the first part of 'aviarius', relating to birds; therefore, it follows, that the grandmother shall be part of a bird. De Vere introduced into the conversation "and no way approve his opinion" so that the Latin 'via', way, can be seen as the basis of both 'avia' and 'aviarius', and therefore 'via' is the soul of 'avia' which inhabits 'aviarius'. There is a triple motto pun in these lines, as 'versare' to think over, is repeated as 'verso'; and Feste repeats "Fare thee well", Latin 'avere' at a greeting or a leave taking, to hail, to bid farewell; which combines with the 'via' of 'avia' and 'aviarius'.

De Vere must have intended the word "still" to take the form of nevertheless, the Latin 'nihilominus', so that he could create the pun on his motto 'aviarius, avia, aviarius, versare, versare, via, avere, nihilominus, aviarius, avia, avere'; and with it we are a long, long way from any possibility of this being merely coincidental.

The Elizabethan nobility could read, write, and speak Latin just as easily as they could read, write, and speak English; and therefore they would have recognised the wit that was hidden not only in these lines, but in almost every line of every play. So just why would William Shakspere of Stratford-upon-Avon want to write plays which contain an average of twenty-six hidden puns on the motto of an English Earl, when he would have known that they would be discovered by the nobility?

When the full diversity and complexity of the punning is recognized in a play, a narrative poem, a song, or a sonnet, it becomes perfectly clear that only the Earl of Oxford could have been the author of the works that have been attributed to William Shakespeare.

An example of how de Vere used the puns on his name and on his motto in a song can be found in the song that brings *Twelfth Night* to a close:

Feste [sings]: When that I was and a little (Latin 'via brevis') tiny boy,

With hey, ho, the wind (Latin 'vertex' a gust
or eddy of wind) and the rain (Latin 'pluvia'),
A foolish (Latin 'devia') thing was but a toy,
For the rain ('pluvia') it raineth eVery day.

In this verse de Vere must have interpreted 'via brevis' as
meaning little, because it would then connect with 'pluvia'
and 'devia'.

But when I came to man's (Latin 'vir') estate,
With hey, ho, the wind ('vertex') and the rain
('pluvia'),
'Gainst (Latin 'adversus') knaves (Latin 'verbero') and thieves men ('viri') shut (French
'verrouiller', to lock, bolt, shut) their gates,
For the rain ('pluvia') it raineth eVery day.

But when I came alas to wife,
With hey, ho, the wind ('vertex') and the rain
('pluvia'),
by swaggering could I neVer thrive (Latin
'virere'),
For the rain ('pluvia') it raineth eVery day.

But when I came unto my beds,
With hey, ho, the wind ('vertex') and the rain
('pluvia'),
With tosspots still ('nihilominus', nevertheless) had drunken (French 'beuverie', drinking) heads (Latin 'vertex' the crown of the
head; or, poetically: the head),
For the rain ('pluvia') it raineth eVery day.

If the word "still" takes the form of nevertheless, it is the
Latin 'nihilominus', and therefore creates a double motto
pun when combined with 'pluvia' rain, which is repeated;
and 'vertex' a gust or eddy of wind, which de Vere interpreted as simply wind and combined with the poetical
meaning of 'vertex': the head. These words form the sym-

metrical motto pun: 'vertex, pluvia, nihilominus, vertex, pluvia'.

> A great while ago the world (Latin 'univer-sum', the whole, which is transferred as meaning the world) began,
> With hey, ho, the wind ('vertex') and the rain ('pluvia'),
> But that's all one (Latin 'nihil interest', it is all one), our play is done (Latin 'absolvere', to bring to a conclusion, to finish),
> And we'll strive (Old French 'estriver') to please you eVery day.

The Latin 'nihil interest', that's all one, does not produce a motto pun in this verse of the song because none of the 'ver' words is repeated, but perhaps it was intended to produce a motto pun with all of the 'ver' words that are repeated in the whole song, and therefore the whole song was intended to identify de Vere as the author, a kind of signature at the end of the play.

Probably an even more interesting example of the use of punning in a song can be found in "It was a loVer and his lass", which I believe is sometimes called "It Ver et Venus", from *As You Like It* (V.iii.). The verse of the song is:

> In springtime (Latin 'vere'), the only pretty ring time,
> When birds do sing (Latin 'aviarius', relating to birds), hey ding a ding, ding,
> Sweet loVers love the spring (Latin 'ver').

The verse is sung four times, repeating the puns on de Vere's name each time, after which Touchstone says:

> Truly (Latin 'vero'), young gentlemen, though there was no great matter in the ditty, yet ('nihilominus') the note was very ('vero' or 'verus') untuneable;

78

which forms the motto pun 'vero, nihilominus, vero'. Touchstone then says:

> By my troth ('vero' in truth), yes ('vero'), I count it but time lost (Latin 'de via decedere', to go astray, to depart from one's course) to hear such a foolish (Latin 'devia') song.

This second line continues the 'vero' pun and combines it with 'de via decedere' and 'devia' to create a double motto pun. The Lewis and Short *Latin Dictionary* says that the Latin word 'devia' can mean foolish, so when Touchstone calls the song foolish, the implication is that it is a 'devia' song, which is to say a de Vere song.

The puns that the Earl of Oxford used are fundamental to the plays and poems of William Shakespeare: everything from the construction of a sentence to the basic outline of a play was governed by de Vere's use of puns on his name and motto. It is known that de Vere as a schoolboy studied Latin for two hours each day and French for two hours each day. It would also seem that he knew Italian because he wrote the Preface to Bartholomew Clarke's translation from Italian to Latin of *The Courtier* by Castiglione when he was twenty-one, and a little later he spent many months in Italy. Ninety per cent of the puns on the Earl of Oxford's name and motto were constructed from Latin, the rest being constructed from French, Italian and a little Spanish. De Vere had known these languages since the earliest years of his life, and therefore they must have been foremost in his mind when he was writing the plays and poems. Indeed, I believe that he was probably thinking simultaneously in English, Latin, French, Italian, and Spanish when writing his plays and poems.

Because the sentences in Shakespeare are sometimes secondary to the puns, understanding the puns makes the sentences more understandable and enjoyable.

Two of the most important scenes in the whole of Shakespeare are the Induction scenes of *The Taming of the Shrew*, though they are rarely performed, probably because their significance is not completely understood today.

In the first of the two scenes a lord comes across a drunk who is sleeping outside an alehouse. The lord has the idea of conveying the drunk to a bedchamber in the lord's house "wrapped in sweet clothes, rings put upon his fingers, a most delicious banquet by his bed and brave attendants near him when he wakes. Would not the beggar then forget himself."

Scene two is the bedchamber in the lord's house. On waking the drunken beggar does not believe that he is a lord, saying: "Am not I Christopher Sly, old Sly's son of Burton Heath, by birth a pedlar, by education a card maker, by transmutation a bearherd, and now by present profession a tinker. Ask Marion Hackett the fat ale wife of Wincot if she knows me not."

William Shakspere's aunt and uncle lived at Barton in the Heath, which is very similar to Burton Heath; and his mother was Mary Arden of Wilmcote, which is also very similar to Wincot. So, in this passage, de Vere identifies the drunken beggar Christopher Sly with William Shakspere of Stratford-upon-Avon.

The lord says to Sly: "Thou art a lord, and nothing but a lord." This is not a pun on de Vere's motto, though it is in the form of a pun; the word lord taking the place of a 'ver' word. The word nothing is used as an abbreviation of the Earl of Oxford's motto, and therefore identifies the lord as the Earl of Oxford.

Sly says: "Upon my life. I am a lord indeed, and not a tinker, nor Christopher Sly". The Latin 'verum' or 'vere' means indeed, so when Sly says "I am a lord indeed" the hidden meaning is 'I am a lord Vere'. A play, *The Taming of the Shrew,* is then performed for the entertainment of Sly (the Latin 'versutus' means sly).

The lord has installed Sly in his own bedchamber. The Latin word for bedchamber is 'cubiculum', which also denotes the emperor's raised seat in the theatre. So Sly is watching the play from the lord's bedchamber, which is also the emperor's raised seat in the theatre.

In these two induction scenes, de Vere is saying that he has given to William Shakspere the life style of a lord. De Vere then goes on to say that he has given Shakspere the emperor's raised seat in the theatre, which in Latin can be transferred as meaning a place of honour in the theatre.

Edward de Vere had written the plays, and it was he who had the place of honour in the theatre, but he gave this place of honour in the theatre to Shakspere by allowing Shakspere to be recognized as the author of his plays. Shakspere was paid to keep quiet, and this is how he acquired the life style of a lord.

It follows from this that, in the plays, whenever there is a drunk, or tinker, or rogue who disguises himself as a lord, and aspires to be a lord, then this character can be identified as representing William Shakspere. Stephano in *The Tempest* is one such character, as is Autolycus in *The Winter's Tale*.

The Earl of Oxford had family connections in and around Stratford-upon-Avon, and it is known that his theatrical company visited the town in 1583 and 1584. It could therefore have been around this time when Oxford first heard of William Shakspere. By the early 1590s Shakspere was preparing to assume the authorship of the plays that had been written by Oxford.

This deception of presenting Shakspere as the author of the plays, the subject of mirth and ridicule until the early years of the seventeenth century, has, since the publication of the First Folio, found increasing acceptance. So much so that today the plays which were written by Edward de Vere have been made to fit the life span of William Shakspere, and the very idea that they could have been written by de Vere is now itself ridiculed on the grounds that he died before the later plays were written.

This point is made by Ian Wilson, in his book *Shakespeare: the Evidence*. However, six pages later, having forgotten that this is his main reason for rejecting Oxford as the author of the plays, he writes: "Equally as daunting is the problem of dating Shakespeare's work, there being hardly a play or poem whose date or composition by Shakespeare is beyond dispute".

Because the plays have been made to fit the life span of Shakspere it has been assumed that they were written in the year of, or a year or two before, the date of publication, registration, or a known performance. In the Elizabethan period many plays were not registered or published until they had been performed for several years and, of course, it is quite absurd to believe that a play was definitely written in the year of a known performance. So the later Shakespeare plays could have been written many years before the presently accepted date of writing.

Edward de Vere died in June 1604 and there are twelve Shakespeare plays which are assumed to have been written in 1604 or later. *Othello* and *Measure for Measure* were performed in November and December 1604 respectively, *Othello* not being published until 1622 and *Measure for Measure* until 1623, so both of these plays could quite easily have been written by de Vere before his death.

King Lear is known to have been performed in 1606 and is therefore assumed to have been written in 1605. A play called *The True Chronicle History of King Leir and his three daughters* was published in 1605 having been entered in the Stationers' Register on 14 May 1594. This play, quite apart from having the title *The True* (Latin 'verus') *Chronicle History*, has, in the scenes which I have read, a marked similarity to the writing style of Shakespeare. This play, according to the *Oxford Shakespeare* "gave Shakespeare much, including suggestions for the characters . . . for the storm . . . and for many details of language". It is therefore not inconceivable that this play is Oxford's earlier version of his Shakespeare play which he re-wrote and which was published in quarto in 1608 as *The True Chronicle History of the life and death of King Lear and his three Daughters*.

The Winter's Tale is based on a romance called *Pandosto, The Triumph of Time* by Robert Greene, which first appeared in 1588. The play could therefore have been written at any time after this date rather than just before a known performance in 1611. At this time the play was entered in the accounts of the Revels as *The Winter's Night's Tale* and a play called *A Wynters nightes pastime* was registered in 1594.

A 'Harry the VIII gown' and a 'Cardinal's gown' can be found in a list of costumes by Edward Alleyn dating from the early 1590s and this could indicate that *Henry VIII* had been written at this time.

A report by Bartholomew Gosnold in 1602 of an expedition sent by the Earl of Southampton to the Elizabeth Islands (Massachusetts) contains many similarities to the description of the island in *The Tempest*. There are also similarities of character and plot between *The Tempest* and *Die Schöne Sidea* by Jacob Ayrer the Elder who died in 1605. So *The Tempest* could have been written between 1602 and 1605.

In 1577 a play called *The Historie of the Solitarie Knight* was presented at Whitehall. The Latin word 'devius' means off the beaten track, out of the way, and is transferred in Latin as meaning living out of the way, solitary. It has been suggested that de Vere wrote this play when out of favour at court and that it is an early version of *Timon of Athens*. In December 1578 a play called *An history of the cruelties of A Stepmother* was performed at court. The Latin 'noverca' means a stepmother and 'novercalis' means of or like a stepmother. This would seem to indicate that this play was also written by de Vere and that he re-wrote it almost twenty years later, calling it *Cymbeline*.

There is no record of an early performance of *Coriolanus* and the play was not published until 1623. The 1607-1609 date of writing is therefore purely conjectural. A play called *Coriolanus tragicomica* appeared in Germany in 1599 and another called *Coriolan* by Alexandre Hardy appeared in 1600. These plays could have been influenced by the Shakespeare play which could have been written and performed some years previously, especially as *Coriolanus* contains twenty-eight motto puns.

The porter's scene in *Macbeth* is said to contain the only reference to a contemporary historical event in the Shakespeare plays. This can be found in the lines:

"Faith, here's an equivocator, that could swear in both the scales against either scale; who committed treason enough for God's sake, yet could not equivocate to heaven: O, come in, equivocator."

which is supposed to reflect the defence of the Jesuit Father Garnet, who was put on trial for having prior knowledge of the Gunpowder Plot. However, these lines might not necessarily refer to Father Garnet's trial because the Jesuit doctrine of equivocation was apparently a standard form of defence.

The Latin word 'tergiversor' means to decline, refuse, to seek a shift or evasion, 'tergiversari' means to equivocate, and 'tergiversator' means one who delays, declines. The porter's lines were therefore constructed from the Latin 'tergiversator, nihilominus, tergiversari, tergiversator' which is a pun on the motto of the Earl of Oxford.

The porter's lines continue:

"I had thought to let in some of all professions, that go the primrose (French 'primevère') way (Latin 'via') to the eVerlasting bonfire (Latin 'avernus', the infernal regions)."

and a few lines later:

"therefore much drink may be said to be an equivocator ('tergiversator') with lechery . . . . in conclusion, equivocates ('tergiversari') him in a sleep, and giving him the lie, leaves him."

So these lines in the porter's scene were constructed from name puns and a motto pun, which shows that they were not connected to the Gunpowder Plot in any way whatsoever as they were written by the Earl of Oxford before his death in 1604.

The equivocator who could not equivocate to heaven must have been Oxford's cousin the Duke of Norfolk who, following the Northern Rebellion of 1569, was executed for the treasonable act of proposing marriage to Mary, Queen of Scots. Norfolk's sister, Jane Howard, was married to the Earl of Westmorland, one of the leaders of the Northern Rebellion and, as she "was a woman of spirit", it is more than likely that she was Oxford's model for Lady Macbeth.

Both *Pericles* and *Antony and Cleopatra* were entered on the Stationers' Register on 20 May 1608. If these plays were performed several years before they were registered, they could have been written before 1604, especially as *Pericles* contains twenty-two motto puns and *Antony and Cleopatra* forty-one.

So the Stratfordians' main objection to Oxford's claim to the authorship is quite easily answered. If, however, the Stratfordians are still convinced that their man is the author of the Shakespeare plays, then they have only to find a rational explanation as to why most of the dialogue is constructed from the clustering of hidden 'ver' words, and why the plays contain an average of twenty-six hidden motto puns.

III

Wordplay in the Poetry

Having read and analysed all of the plays, I decided to re-read the narrative poems, finding eight motto puns in *Venus and Adonis*, and twelve motto puns in *The Rape of Lucrece*.

The opening stanzas of *Venus and Adonis* are concerned with the horse, the colour red, the rose, the lips, and kissing; as follows:

> Here come and sit, where neVer serpent hisses,
> And being set, I'll smother thee with kisses (Latin 'savia');
> And yet ('nihilominus') not cloy the lips (Old English 'vermeil', a scarlet or red colour, frequently applying to the lips) with loathed saiety,
> but rather famish them amid their plenty,
> Making them red (Old English 'vermeil', red or scarlet) and pale with fresh (Latin 'virere') variety (Latin 'varietas' or 'diversitas');
> Ten kisses short as one, one long as twenty (Latin 'savia', kisses).

These lines were constructed from the repeating of the

Latin 'savia' and the Old English 'vermeil', which, when combined with the Latin 'nihilominus' create the double motto pun 'savia, nihilominus, vermeil, vermeil, savia'.

The Old French word vermilion, which is derived from 'vermeil', means a blush; the Latin phrase 'verecundus oris' also means a blush, and 'verecundia' means a feeling of shame; therefore, de Vere connected a blush with shame in the succeeding stanzas:

> Over one arm the lusty courser's (Latin 'veredus', a swift horse) rein,
> Under her other was the tender boy,
> Who blushed (Old French 'vermilion' or Latin 'verecundus oris') and pouted in a dull disdain
> . . . .
> She red (Old English 'vermeil') and hot as coals of glowing fire,
> He red ('vermeil') for shame ('verecundia'), but frosty in desire (Latin 'avere' to desire) . . . .
> Now doth she stroke his cheek (Old French 'vermilion', painting the body, especially the cheeks, a bright red or scarlet), now doth he frown,
> And 'gins to chide, but soon she stops his lips ('vermeil', red, of the lips) . . . .
> He burns with bashful (Latin 'verecundus') shame ('verecundia'); she with her tears
> Doth quench the maiden (Latin 'virgo') burning of his cheeks (Old French 'vermilion') . . . .
> He saith she is immodest ('inverecundus'), blames her miss;
> What follows more she murders with a kiss (Latin 'savium': a kiss).

So it can be seen that these lines were constructed from the Old English word 'vermeil', which means red or scarlet colour, frequently applying to the lips; the Old French word 'vermilion', which means a blush, the painting of the body, especially the cheeks; the Latin 'verecundus oris', which also means a blush; 'verecundia', which means a feeling of shame; 'verecundus", which means bashful; 'inverecundus', which means immodest; and 'savium' a kiss; all of which are connected and interrelated to each other.

Similar connections in the painting of the Troy episode from *The Rape of Lucrece* form a motto pun. The episode begins at line 1366 as follows:

> At last she calls to mind where hangs a piece
> of skilful painting, made for Priam's Troy . . . .
> Which the conceited painter drew so proud
> As heaven, it seemed, to kiss the turrets.bowed.
>
> A thousand lamentable objects there,
> In scorn of nature ('veritas'), art gave lifeless life
> ('imitari veritatem'):

So the whole of this episode could be interpreted as having been constructed from the Latin phrase 'imitari veritatem', to imitate life in works of art. The pun on the motto begins at line 1457 and covers two stanzas:

> On this sad shadow Lucrece spends her eyes,
> And shapes her sorrow to the beldam's (Latin 'avia', a grandmother) woes (Latin 'res adversae'),
> Who nothing ('nihil') wants to answer (Latin 'respondere adversus', to answer) her but cries,
> And bitter words to ban her cruel foes ('adversarii', antagonists from 'adversarius', an opponent):
> The painter was no good to lend her those;
> And therefore Lucrece swears (Latin 'in certa verba iurare') he did her wrong (Latin 'perversus', wrong or wrong doing),
> To give her so much grief and not a tongue.
> 'Poor instrument', quoth she, 'without a sound,
> I'll tune thy woes ('res adversae') with my lamenting tongue,
> And drop sweet balm in Priam's painted wound (Latin 'vulnus adversum', a wound in the front),

And rail on (Italian 'inveire', to rail against)
Pyrrhus that hath done him wrong ('perversus',
wrong doing),
And with my tears quench Troy that burns so
long,
And with my knife scratch out the angry (Latin
'iratus adversus', anger or angry towards) eyes
Of all the Greeks that are thine enemies ('adversarii').

Now that we know how de Vere constructed his lines
it seems quite logical that the anger should be
directed towards "all the Greeks that are thine enemies",
because the Latin 'ira adversus' is connected to
'adversarii'.

The main motto pun in these lines was created by
combining the clustering of 'adversus', and its derivations,
with 'nihil'. However, if de Vere interpreted "bitter words"
as the Latin 'acerba verba', then 'verba' was also repeated
with the phrase 'in certa verba iurare'. It then follows that
"to answer" becomes a pivotal verb in these lines, because
it connects the 'adversus' segment with the 'verba' segment as both 'respondere adversus' and 'ut verba verbis
respondeant' can be interpreted as meaning to answer.
Another word that is repeated is 'perversus', and therefore these lines form a multiple-word motto pun.

It is interesting that in his plays and poems the Earl
of Oxford frequently combined the word outward with the
word inward; as at line 1544 of *The Rape of Lucrece*:

To me came Tarquin armed too beguiled
With outward honesty, but yet ('nihilominus')
defiled
With inward vice . . .

The French phrase 'vers l'extérieur' means outward, and
'vers l'intérieur' means inward, therefore these lines were
constructed around the words 'vers l'extérieur, nihilominus, vers l'intérieur'; which form a motto pun.

Other words which de Vere invariably combined are winter and summer, as in the opening lines of *Richard III*:

Now is the winter of our discontent
Made glorious summer by this sun of York . . .

The Italian word 'inverno' means winter, and the Spanish word 'verano' means summer.

I then read and analysed all of the sonnets. Many were created around themes which have been developed from 'ver' words of phrases. Edward de Vere had taken a 'ver' word or phrase, translated it into English, extended its meaning, and then created a sonnet around the extended meaning of the 'ver' word. An example would be the Latin phrase 'verus cantus', the literal meaning of which is a true song, but which is transferred, in Latin, as meaning a prediction. Sonnet 14 revolves around predictions, the telling of fortunes, the stars and astronomy, which in Latin is 'astrologia', and prognostication. The whole of the sonnet has been created around the Latin phrase 'verus cantus', which is a name pun.

Another example, and perhaps the most important in the sonnets, is the Latin word 'avere', which means to wish, to desire, to crave, to long for. When the word will is used as meaning wish or desire, as in "What is your will?", then will can also be interpreted as being 'avere'. Edward de Vere created two sonnets, 135 and 136, from the word 'avere'. The opening line of sonnet 135 is:

"Whoever hath her wish, thou hast thy Will".

The words wish and Will have both been translated from 'avere'. As de Vere was writing puns, any and every form of the word will, including the name Will, was interpreted by him as being the Latin word 'avere'.

In sonnet 135 de Vere used 'avere' fourteen times, translated as Will, will, and wish. In sonnet 136 he used 'avere' seven times, and combined them with the word nothing, the Latin 'nihil', to create a motto pun. The last two lines of sonnet 136 are:

"Make but my name thy love, and love that still
And then thou lov'st me, for my name is Will."

The underlying meaning of "for my name is Will" is "for my name is 'avere' "; and 'avere' or 'a vere' can only be Edward de Vere. Among his literary and theatrical friends, Edward de Vere, the seventeenth Earl of Oxford was probably known as "Will".

As with the lines of the Chorus in *Henry V*, the theme of sonnet 44 was constructed from the Latin word 'advertere', which in Latin can be transferred as meaning of thoughts, as follows:

If the dull substance of my flesh were thought ('advertere'),
Injurious distance should not stop my way (Latin 'via') . . . .
For nimble thought ('advertere') can jump both sea and land
As soon as think ('versare' to think) the place where he should be
But ah, thought ('advertere') kills me that I am not thought ('advertere'),
To leap large lengths of miles when thou art gone
. . . .

The spark of invention for sonnet 57 is the Latin word 'servire' meaning to serve. This can be seen in the opening lines:

Being your slave ('servire', to be a slave) what should I do but tend ('servire', to serve),
Upon your hours, and times of your desire ('avere', to desire)?
I have no precious time at all to spend;
Nor services ('servitii' from 'servire') to do till you require;

this is followed by:

> Nor dare I question with my jealous thought
> (Latin 'advertere', to turn, of thought),
> Where you may be, or your affairs suppose,
> But like a sad slave ('servire') stay and think
> (Latin 'versare', to think over) of nought ('nihil')
> Save where you are, how happy you make those.
> So true a fool is love, that in your will ('avere'),
> Though you do anything, he thinks ('versare') no
> ill.

So the whole sonnet could be interpreted as being a triple motto pun because it was constructed from the repeating of the Latin words 'servire', 'avere', 'versare' with 'advertere', which were all combined with 'nihil'.

The predominant word in sonnet 116 is 'convertere', combined with 'versare' and 'in errore versari'. There are however other interesting aspects to this sonnet, as follows:

> Let me not to the marriage of true ('verus') minds
> Admit impediments, love is not love
> Which alters ('convertere' to alter) when it alteration ('conversio') finds,
> Or bends ('versare' to bend) with the remoVer to remove ('removere').
> O no, it is an eVer fixed mark
> That looks on tempests and is neVer shaken
> (Latin 'commovere', to shake);
> It is the star to eVery wandering bark,
> Whose worth's unknown, although his height be taken (Latin 'vertex', the pole of the heavens, the highest, the uttermost).
> Love's not Time's fool, though rosy (French 'vermeil', red) lips and cheeks (Old French 'vermeil', red, of the lips and cheeks)
> Within his bending ('versare' to bend) sickle's compass come,

Love alters ('convertere') not with his brief hours and weeks,
But bears it out even to the edge of doom:
If this be error ('in errore versari', to be mistaken) and upon me proved,
I neVer writ (Italian 'scrivere' to write), nor no man ('vir') eVer loved.

It is clear that in this sonnet the star is the pole star, the star that is true and constant; and that this star must be the star that can be seen on the de Vere shield because his motto is 'Truly nothing truer'. The Latin 'deviare' means to wander, and is derived from the word 'devia', which means wandering about in unfrequented places. The hidden meaning of this line is that love is the de Vere star to eVery devia bark! The conclusion of the sonnet is that if this is proved to be an error, then no man, no 'vir', no de Vere, eVer loved.

To whom was de Vere directing his true and constant love? I have referred to sonnet 3 and to the recipient being his "mother's glass", to the French word 'verre' being a glass, and to the hidden meaning being that "Thou art thy mother's 'verre', thy mother's de Vere", that Edward de Vere was saying "Thou art my son". The sonnet begins:

Look (the Spanish 'ver', to see, to look) in thy glass (the French 'verre', glass) . . . .

It is interesting that 'Shakespeare' hardly ever used the word mirror, but almost always the word glass. Perhaps this is because the French word for a mirror is either 'miroir' or 'glace', neither of them a pun on the name of de Vere, whereas the word 'verre' is a name pun.

Sonnet 77 begins with the same word:

Thy glass (French 'verre') will show thee how thy beauties wear . . . .

and continues with:

> The wrinkles which thy glass ('verre') will truly
> (Latin 'vero') show . . . ."

the 'verre' and the 'vero' implying that the object of de Vere's affection was also a de Vere.

It becomes more than an implication, and more than coincidence, when the subject of the sonnets is frequently referred to as being true or as being truly fair, as in sonnet 82:

> yet when they have devised
> What strained touches rhetoric can lend,
> Thou, truly (Latin 'vero') fair (Southern Middle
> English 'veir'), wert truly ('vero') sympathized
> In true ('verus') plain words by thy true-telling
> friend ('amicus verus') . . . .

De Vere was the true-telling friend to the truly fair; the father to the son.

In sonnet 85 we read:

> Hearing you praised I say, ' 'Tis so, 'tis true
> ('verus')'.

So the praise that was given to the object of de Vere's affection was true, which yet again implies that this person was 'true' and was therefore a de Vere. Incidentally, the whole of this sonnet was constructed from the Latin 'advertere' of thoughts; together with the Latin 'verbum' a word or phrase; 'verba', words; and 'orationem satis multis verbis', to praise very highly.

But de Vere's son was not only referred to as being 'true'; in sonnet 1 we find:

> Thou that art now the world's fresh (Latin 'virere'
> to be fresh) ornament
> And only herald to the gaudy spring . . . .

and in sonnet 63:

And all those beauties whereof now he's king
Are vanishing (Latin 'defectio virium', a vanishing) or vanished out of sight,
Stealing away (Latin 'subducere viatica', to steal
away) the treasure of his spring . . . .

both of which connect him with the spring. The Latin
word 'ver' means spring, and 'vere' can mean in the
springtime.

Once it is realized that the sonnets were written by
Edward de Vere, and that the object of de Vere's affections
was his son, the solution to the puzzle that is presented in
sonnet 22 is not too difficult to find:

My glass ('verre') shall not persuade me I am old
So long as youth and thou are of one date . . . .
For all the beauty that doth cover thee
Is but the seemly raiment of my heart,
Which in thy brest doth live, as thine in me.
How can I then be elder than thou art?

and the enigmatic aspects of sonnet 62 are quite easily
resolved:

But when my glass ('verre') shews me myself
indeed (Latin 'vere'),
Beated and chopped with tanned antiquity,
Mine own self love quite contrary (Latin 'adver-
sus') I read –
Self so self loving were iniquity:
'Tis thee, myself, that for myself I praise,
Painting my age with beauty of thy days.

The same sentiments are expressed in sonnet 39:

What can mine own praise to mine own self bring,
And what is't but my own when I praise thee?

In sonnet 103 it is clear that when the son looks in his glass he will see his father:

> For to no other pass my Verses tend
> Than of your graces and your gifts to tell;
> And more, much more, than in my Verse can sit,
> Your own glass ('verre') shows you when you look
> (Spanish 'ver') in it.

Finally the line in sonnet 92: "For term of life thou art assured mine;" can only be a father writing to a son.

The two narrative poems *Venus and Adonis* and *The Rape of Lucrece* were dedicated to Henry Wriothesley, Earl of Southampton, and therefore many commentators have assumed that the Earl of Southampton must have been Shakespeare's patron. Following on from this it has been assumed that the object of Shakespeare's affection in the sonnets is also Henry Wriothesley because "the onlie begetter", or inspiration, of the sonnets was "Mr. W.H."; which are the reversed initials of Henry Wriothesley.

I think the opening lines of sonnet 95 are the key to the problem of just who was the object of Shakespeare's affections:

> How sweet and lovely dost thou make the shame
> (Latin 'verecundia')
> Which, like a canker in the fragrant rose,
> Doth spot the beauty of thy budding name!

I have read that in the name Wriothesley, the 'i' was pronounced and the 'o' was silent, which gives the pronunciation Risley. However, if the 'o' was pronounced and the 'i' was silent in the Elizabethan period the pronunciation would have been Rosley or Roseley, and would therefore have been a 'budding name'. Shame, the Latin word 'verecundia', spots the beauty of Roseley like a canker in the rose. The hidden meaning must be that Henry Wriothesley was illegitimate and that it was the name of his father, de Vere, which was a "shame" to the "beauty of thy budding name".

In sonnet 67 we read:

> Why should false painting imitate (Latin 'imitari veritatem' of works of art) his cheek . . . .
> Why should poor beauty indirectly seek
> Roses of shadows since his rose is true ('verus')?

meaning: since his Roseley is de Vere!

Just as de Vere used the words true, truth, and nothing from his motto to identify himself symbolically, so also I believe he used the words one and all, from the Earl of Southampton's motto of 'One for all, all for one', to identify Henry Wriothesley. As for example in sonnet 105:

> Since all alike my songs and praises be
> To one, of one, still such, and ever so . . . .
> Fair, kind, and true ('verus') have often lived alone,
> Which three till now never kept in one.

and in sonnet 109:

> For nothing ('nihil') this wide world I call,
> Save thou my rose; in it thou art my all.

both the rose and the all representing Henry Wriothesley.

In sonnet 8 de Vere is urging Wriothesley to marry and produce children:

> Mark (Latin 'animadvertere') how one string, sweet husband (Latin 'vir') to another,
> Strikes ('verberare') each in each by mutual ordering,
> Resembling (Latin 'verisimilis', resembling) sire, and child, and happy mother,
> Who all in one one pleasing note do sing (Latin 'cantare convivia', to celebrate in singing).

The "all in one" are the two symbolical words that represent the Earl of Southampton.

It appears to me that the evidence in the sonnets that the Earl of Southampton was the son of the Earl of Oxford is fairly conclusive though not absolutely overwhelming. If Henry Wriothesley was the son of Edward de Vere, the question which then has to be asked is: who was his mother? Perhaps there is a clue in the sonnet which gives the clue as to how de Vere constructed his plays and poems: sonnet 76, and in the line:

Why write I still all one, ever the same . . . .

As has been noted, "all one" probably implies the Earl of Southampton and, because the sonnet was constructed from the Latin word 'verbum' and combined with 'nihilominus' to create a motto pun, the whole sonnet implies the Earl of Oxford. The phrase "ever the same" could also imply E.Vere the same; but it could also be a translation of Elizabeth I's motto "Semper Eadem" Always, or ever, the same. So in this one line the Earl of Southampton can be connected to the Earl of Oxford and Elizabeth I.

At a pageant in May 1582, four knights representing "Desire" attacked the "Castle of Perfect Beauty", which was presumably a symbol of virginity and therefore a representation of Elizabeth I. The pageant was held during the period when there were proposals for the Duke of Anjou to marry Elizabeth. However, the "Castle of Perfect Beauty" was not overthrown by "Desire".

The Faerie Queene by Edmund Spenser was dedicated to Elizabeth I and, in a letter of 1589, Spenser wrote: "For considering she beareth two persons, the one of a most royall Queene or Empresse, the other of a most vertuous and beautiful lady, this latter part in some places I do express in Belphoebe . . . .".

During the years of the Cult of Gloriana poets represented Elizabeth I with all aspects of virginity and, although she was not physically beautiful, she was often called beautiful. Perhaps beautiful was used by the poets as a discreet alternative to virginal; and beauty, like the "Castle of Perfect Beauty", was a tactful reference to Elizabeth's virginity.

The Latin 'vero' means not only truly, but also in truth, and so if the word "truth" represents the Earl of Oxford and the word "beauty" represents Elizabeth I, sonnet 14 has some very significant implications.

As noted earlier this sonnet was constructed from the Latin words 'veridici cantus', a prophecy; and 'verum cantare', to predict, but as the sonnet develops the meaning of the lines become more significant:

> But from thine eyes my knowledge I derive,
> And, constant stars, in them I read such art ('imitari veritatem')
> As truth ('vero') and beauty shall together thrive (Latin 'virere', to thrive)
> If from thyself to store thou wouldst convert (Latin 'convertere');
> Or else of thee this I prognosticate ('veridici cantus'):
> Thy end is truth and beauty's doom and date.

Which can now be interpreted as meaning that if the Earl of Southampton would marry and have children, then the Earl of Oxford and Elizabeth I would thrive; but if he were not to marry and have children there would be no descendants of the Earl of Oxford and Elizabeth I.

Sonnet 99 was constructed from the Latin 'intervertere', which means to intercept and therefore to embezzle, rob, purloin, cheat. However the real significance of the sonnet can now be seen in the lines:

> The purple pride
> Which on thy soft cheek for complexion dwells
> In my love's veins thou hast too grossly dyed.

The purple pride represents the royal purple which is in

the Earl of Southampton's veins. In other words the Earl of Southampton has royal blood and because of this he has been conspicuously wronged, presumably by not being recognized as heir to the throne. The sonnet continues:

> The roses fearfully on thorns did stand,
> One blushing ('verecundus oris') shame ('verecundia'), another white despair;
> A third, nor red nor white, had stol'n of both,

This would be the red and white of the Tudor rose.

> And to his robbery had annexed thy breath,
> But for his theft in pride of all his growth
> A vengeful canker eat him up to death.

The line of succession of the Tudors will end with Elizabeth's death.

If the Earl of Southampton was the son of the Earl of Oxford and Elizabeth I, why would it have been so important to keep it a secret? I believe that the answer lies in Elizabeth's determination to unite the Protestant and Catholic factions in the country. The Earl of Southampton could not be recognized as the successor to Elizabeth because he was illegitimate and James VI of Scotland was the rightful successor. Even to acknowledge him as the illegitimate son of Elizabeth would have caused a war with Scotland and civil war in England. It remained therefore of paramount importance to maintain the lie that Elizabeth was a virgin, even by going so far as to glorify her virginity. The Virgin Queen became a counter-balance to the Virgin Mary, and a unifying force for the country.

In the light of these political considerations it becomes possible to understand, and to have some sympathy for, Edward de Vere when he wrote these lines in sonnet 36:

> I may not evermore acknowledge thee,
> Lest my bewailéd guilt should do thee shame;

Nor thou with public kindness honour me,
Unless thou take that honour from thy name.
But do not so; I love thee in such sort
As, thou being mine, mine is thy good report.

It follows from this that Edward de Vere, seventeenth Earl of Oxford, could never be recognized as being the author of the plays and poems attributed to William Shakespeare because, if he had been, someone would have realized the real significance of the characters in his plays and, when they were published in 1609 after his death, the lines in his sonnets.

Edward de Vere knew that he was an immortal poet, but he also realized that he would never be acknowledged as such, and that he would be forgotten; as sonnet 81 testifies:

The earth can yield me but a common grave,
When you entombéd in men's eyes shall lie:
Your monument shall be my gentle verse,
Which eyes not yet created shall o'er read.

And sonnet 55:

Not marble, nor the gilded monuments
Of princes shall outlive this powerful rhyme;
But you shall shine more bright in these contents
Than unswept stone besmeared with sluttish time.

And sonnet 72, which concludes with a motto pun:

O, lest your true love may seem false in this,
That you for love speak well of me untrue,
My name be buried where my body is
And live no more to shame ('verecundia') nor me nor you.
For I am shamed ('verecundia') by that which I bring forth,

And so should you, to love things nothing ('nihil')
worth.

The name of Shakespeare in the shape of William
Shakspere of Stratford-upon-Avon lives on, which shows
that had William Shakspere been Shakespeare he was
mistaken in his belief that his name would be buried with
his body. However, the real Shakespeare was not mistak-
en in his belief that his verse would be immortal but he
would be forgotten, because the real Shakespeare was
Edward de Vere, who, for almost four hundred years, has
been forgotten.

IV

Marlowe and Lyly

All the plays, sonnets, narrative poems, and the shorter poems that have been attributed to William Shakespeare were written by Edward de Vere. However there is, apparently, a group of people who believe that these works were written by Christopher Marlowe, because there is a similarity of style between the writing of William Shakespeare and the writing of Marlowe. *The Dictionary of National Biography* says: "Shakespeare's earlier style often closely resembles his (Marlowe's), and it is not at all times possible to distinguish the two with certainty". This is followed by: "All the blank verse in Shakespeare's early plays bear the stamp of Marlowe's inspiration". In his biography *Christopher Marlowe*, A. L. Rowse wrote: "Shakespeare's subconscious mind was drenched in Marlowe, and from first to last threw up a rainbow-spray."

The Marlovians also believe that Marlowe wrote the works of Shakespeare because, in the accepted chronology of the plays, Marlowe was writing before Shakespeare. However, the Earl of Oxford was Shakespeare, and started writing plays about 1576, eleven or twelve years before Marlowe's first play. If the Marlovians believe that Marlowe had written the plays of Shakespeare because

Marlowe came before Shakespeare, could not the Earl of Oxford, who was Shakespeare, have written the plays of Marlowe because he came before Marlowe? If the Earl of Oxford had not only written the plays of Shakespeare but also the plays of Marlowe it would certainly account for the similarity of the writing, and would also tie up everything very neatly.

When I had glanced briefly at *Doctor Faustus* previously, I had noted a similarity between the rhythm of *Doctor Faustus* and the rhythm of the plays attributed to Shakespeare. I had also noted a similarity in the use of words.

Edward de Vere had occasionally used name puns in the titles of the Shakespeare plays. I found an entry for 'faustus' in my Latin dictionary. It means faVourable, lucky; and is derived from 'favere', to faVour.

I started to read *Doctor Faustus* cautiously, having an open mind as to whether it had been written by de Vere.

There are two texts of *Doctor Faustus*, the first published in 1604, the year of de Vere's death and eleven years after Marlowe's death. The second text was published in 1616, the year of William Shakspere's death. According to one academic, the second text of 1616 adds to the first text of 1604, for the most part, only the light, simple-minded comedy of the clowns. Another academic says that in this tomfoolery of the clowns, not only does the play lose its way, but Marlowe also lost his way. The academics seem to agree that the tomfoolery of the clowns is poor writing and detracts from the intellectual qualities of the rest of the play. It was however this tomfoolery that first convinced me that *Doctor Faustus* had been written by de Vere.

One of the clowns, Robin the hostler, aspires to being a conjuror like Doctor Faustus, and can be seen as being a character who tries to become the master, like Christopher Sly, Autolycus, and Stephano. He therefore represents William Shakspere. In Latin, 'praestigiator' means a juggler; 'praestigiae' means juggling, deception; and 'praestigis uti' means to perform conjuring tricks.

With the words from his books Doctor Faustus can conjure up historical figures from the dead. The Latin phrase 'praestigiae verborum', which is a pun on de Vere's name, means the deceptive use of words; which was how de Vere interpreted Faustus' conjuring up of historical figures with the words from his books.

Faustus, like Prospero, whose art is magic, represents de Vere the dramatist, who, with words, conjures up historical figures in the magical world of the theatre.

The other clowns, who also represent Shakspere, are a carter; from the Latin 'vehere' to carry by carriage; and a horse courser, Latin 'veredus' a horse; or 'veredarius' the rider of a post horse, a courier. The horse courser ('veredarius') buys a horse ('veredus') from Doctor (Latin 'vir doctus' a learned man) Faustus (favourable) for less than Faustus' valuation of the horse ('veredus'). The horse courser ('veredarius') ignores Faustus' advice that he should not ride ('vehere') the horse ('veredus') into water, saying: "I, thinking the horse ('veredus') had some quality that he would not have me know of, what did I but ride ('vehere') him into a great riVer ('fluvius'), and when I came just in the midst, my horse ('veredus') vanished away, and I sat straddling upon a bottle of hay".

In the Elizabethan period the feed for a horse was a bottle or bundle of hay. The Latin word 'manipulus' means a small bundle, but is transferred as meaning a company of foot soldiers because, in early Roman times, the standard of a company of foot soldiers was a pole with a bundle of hay at the top. So by straddling upon a bundle of hay the implication is that the horse courser is straddling upon a company of foot soldiers. The Latin word 'vir' was a military technical term for a foot soldier, and so a bundle of hay is a witty indirect pun on de Vere's name.

The whole of the horse courser's story is repeated in the play and, far from losing his way, de Vere knew exactly what he was doing. He repeated the story so that he could repeat the Latin 'ver' words 'veredarius', 'veredus', 'vehere', 'fluvius', the pun on a bundle of hay, 'vir'; and by so doing he drives home the point, for those who could understand his wit, that he had written the play.

The simple light-hearted comedy of the clowns is de Vere's way of trying to have some kind of literary revenge on William Shakspere. In the play Robin does not succeed in becoming a conjuror, just as Stephano does not succeed in obtaining Prospero's magical mantle; and the horse courser does not obtain Faustus's horse, his 'veredus', his 'veres', his plays.

The clowns are each in turn charmed dumb, unable to speak, just as Shakspere never spoke or wrote anything concerning his authorship of the plays because he was paid to stay dumb.

The story of William Shakespeare being the holder of horses outside London theatres probably had its origins in *Doctor Faustus*, as well as in the story of Mine Host of the Garter in *The Merry Wives of Windsor*.

I have found thirty puns on the Earl of Oxford's motto in *Doctor Faustus*, which is more than the average number of puns in the 'Shakespeare' plays.

An example of a motto pun from *Doctor Faustus* can be found in Act I, Scene iii:

Faustus: Did not my conjuring speeches ('praestigiae verborum') raise thee? Speak ('verba facere').

Mephistopheles: That was the cause, but yet ('nihilominus') *per accidens*; for when we hear one rack the name of God, abjure ('verbis conceptis periurare') the scriptures and his saViour Christ ('verbigena'), we fly in hope to get his soul . . . . Therefore the shortest cut for conjuring ('praestigiae verborum') is stoutly to abjure ('verbis conceptis periurare') all godliness and pray devoutly to the prince of hell ('avernus', the infernal regions).

These lines were constructed from 'praestigiae verborum', the deceptive use of words, 'verba facere', to speak, 'verbigena', which *A Latin Dictionary* by Lewis and Short translates as: He who was born of the word, Christ; and the repeating of 'verbis conceptis periurare' to forswear oneself; all derivations of 'verbum'. Because the Latin 'verbo' can mean in name or in word it is also probable that de Vere interpreted name as being 'verbo'. When these words are combined with 'nihilominus' a witty little motto pun is created.

It cannot be emphasized too strongly that the clustering of 'ver' words, combined with 'nihil' or 'nihilominus', and the repeating of two, three, four, or more of these 'ver' words, combined with 'nihil' or 'nihilominus', does not appear in every single play that was written during the Elizabethan and early Jacobean periods, and therefore these motto puns cannot be explained away as being simply coincidental or normal Elizabethan English usage. The plays in which these complex motto puns appear must have been written by the Earl of Oxford.

The plays attributed to Christopher Marlowe contain an average of twenty-one puns on the Earl of Oxford's motto, as well as the same diversity of name puns as can be found in the 'Shakespeare' plays.

In *Edward II* (V.ii.71), Queen Isabella say: "Commend me humbly to his majesty, and tell him that I labour all in vain to ease his grief and work his liberty", and in the following scene Matrevis says: "Why strive you thus? Your labour is in vain". In *Dido, Queen of Carthage* Anna says: "Alas, poor king, that labours so in vain for her that so delighteth in thy pain". These lines were constructed from the Latin 'sulcos in pulvere ducere', to labour in vain; and this same Latin phrase was also the basis for the title of *Love's Labour's Lost*, to labour in vain being interpreted as "labour's lost".

In *Edward II* (V.iv.) there is an interesting episode in which Lightborn says:

> 'Tis not the first time I have kill'd a nan ('vir').
> I learned in Naples how to poison ('virulentus', full of poison, poisonous, virulent) flowers,
> To strangle ('intercludere viam', to choke) with a

lawn thrust down the throat ('via', the gullet),
To pierce ('transverberare', to pierce through) the
windpipe ('via') with a needle's point,
Or, whilst one is asleep, to take a quill, and blow
a little powder ('pulverius', of or belonging to
dust, from 'pulvis', dust, powder) in his ears ('via'
any passage),
Or open his mouth ('via' any passage), and pour
quick-silVer down.
But yet ('nihilominus') I have a braVer way ('via').

These lines were constructed from the repeating of 'via'
which, when combined with 'nihilominus' created a motto
pun.

Elizabeth I is reported as saying: "I am Richard II,
know ye not that?". *Edward II is*, like *Richard II*, an alle-
gory, and was written as a warning of what could happen
in England if Elizabeth were to be deposed. Some commentators have suggested that the character of Gaveston
represents the author, and therefore the first part of the
play can now be interpreted as representing the relationship between Elizabeth and the Earl of Oxford.

Only the *Tamberlaine* plays, of those attributed to
Christopher Marlowe, were printed during Marlowe's life-
time, and these plays were printed anonymously. *The
Dictionary of National Biography* says: "The only external
contemporary testimony to Marlowe's authorship of the
piece is a reference to Marlowe under the pseudonym of
Tamberlaine in 1593". This would be Gabriel Harvey's
Newe letter of Notable Contents, written in September
1593, in which he wrote that death, "smiling at his
Tamberlaine contempt", is declared to have "struck home
this peremptory stroke". Therefore, during his lifetime,
Christopher Marlowe was not known as the writer of the
plays that have been attributed to him. Similarly, the first
fifteen or sixteen of the plays attributed to William
Shakespeare were also printed anonymously. It was only
in 1598 that Francis Meres revealed that Shakespeare,
not even William Shakespeare, had written twelve of

Author says Earl of Oxford wrote Marlowe plays not vice versa —

these plays. Christopher Marlowe did not write the plays *include* that have been attributed to Christopher Marlowe, just as *Faustus* William Shakspere did not write the plays that have been attributed to William Shakespeare. There is just as much of the Earl of Oxford's hidden wit in the plays of Marlowe as there is in the plays of Shakespeare.

The problem of why particular phrases, aspects of plots, and the general writing styles of William Shakespeare and Christopher Marlowe are so similar is finally resolved. The plays, narrative poems, sonnets and shorter poems of William Shakespeare, together with the plays and the narrative poem of Christopher Marlowe were all in fact written by the same man: Edward de Vere, seventeenth Earl of Oxford.

It wasn't enough for Edward de Vere simply to hide behind a pseudonym, because people would naturally become inquisitive about the actual author, and his identity would probably have been revealed to the nation. As one of the premier Earls of all England, closely associated with Elizabeth I and the son-in-law of her Principal Secretary of State, Lord Burghley, he had to find a real live person who would assume the authorship of the plays and poems that he had written.

If it had become known that the Earl of Oxford had written the plays, then the nation at large would have realized that many characters in the plays represented not only various aspects of de Vere himself but also Elizabeth I and Lord Burghley. From this, a close relationship between the Earl of Oxford and Elizabeth I might have been imagined, the consequences of which could have been catastrophic for the security of the monarchy and the country. It is therefore quite possible that Elizabeth and Lord Burghley may only have allowed the Earl of Oxford to write the plays on condition that he was never, in any circumstances, to be revealed as the author.

John Lyly was the first person to assume the authorship of the plays written by the Earl of Oxford. The Blackfriars Theatre had been leased by Oxford, who had made his secretary, John Lyly, the manager. Lyly was therefore readily accepted as being the author of the plays that had been played by the Earl of Oxford's boys' company at the Blackfriars Theatre.

The Euphuism in these plays was created by the joining together of the puns on de Vere's name so that, when they were translated into English, the language became like a cluster of mixed metaphors and similes. The Latin 'compages' means a joining together, a structure, and is therefore used when referring to the structure of the body, the anatomy. The book *Euphues – An Anatomy of Wyt* written in 1578 by John Lyly, is a joining together, a connecting of wit, and the plays of John Lyly were constructed in exactly the same way: the wit being the puns on de Vere's name. Those Euphuistic writers who are thought of as being imitators of Lyly were in fact imitators of the Earl of Oxford's early method of joining together puns on his name, Oxford's style of writing in his Shakespeare plays being merely a more subtle and sophisticated variation of his style of writing in his earlier 'Lyly' plays.

This passage from *Endimion* (I.i.), has been cited as an example of 'Lyly's' euphuism:

> Oh fair Cynthia, why do others term thee unconstant (Latin 'devia', inconstant) whom I have eVer found unmoveable? Injurious time, corrupt manners (Latin 'via', manner), unkind men, who, finding a constancy not to be matched in my sweet mistress, have christened her with the name waVering, waxing and waning. Is she inconstant ('devia') that keepeth a settled course ('via'), which since her first creation altereth ('convertere', to alter) not one minute in her moving ('movere', to move)?
>
> There is nothing ('nihil') thought ('advertere', of thought) more admirable or commendable in the sea than the ebbing and flowing ('fluvius', flowing water); and shall the moon, from whom the sea taketh this virtue ('virtus'), be accounted fickle for increasing and decreasing? Flowers in their buds

Othello, Winter's Tale, others of husband falsely accusing wife of infidelity wrongly (to cover up wife's indiscretion)

are nothing ('nihil') worth till they be blown, nor
blossoms accounted till they be ripe fruit; and
shall we then say they be changeable ('versabilis')
. . . .

These lines were constructed from the repeating of 'via'
with 'devia' and 'fluvius', and 'convertere' with 'versabilis',
which were combined with the repeating of 'nihil' to form
a double motto pun. The passage continues:

> Tell me, Eumenides, what is he that having a
> mistress of ripe years and infinite virtues ('vir-
> tus'), great honours and unspeakable beauty, but
> would wish ('avere') that she might grow tender
> again, getting youth by years, and never decaying
> beauty by time, whose fair face neither the sum-
> mer's (Spanish 'verano') blaze can scorch nor win-
> ter's (Italian 'inverno') chap, nor the numbering of
> years breed altering of colours ('versicolor', chang-
> ing colour)? Such is my sweet Cynthia . . . .

Cynthia, the Moon Queen, was an alternative name for
Diana, the virgin goddess of the Moon, as well as being an
alternative name for Spenser's Belphoebe. Therefore the
Moon is one of the symbolical representations of virginity
and Elizabeth I. Most of the characters in the play represent different aspects of the Earl of Oxford and Elizabeth
I. For example Endimion represents the public face of the
Earl of Oxford and Cynthia represents Elizabeth the
monarch, whereas Eumenides represents the private Earl
of Oxford, and Tellus together with Semele represent
Elizabeth the woman.

Tellus, the "flower of beauty, which is honoured in
courts" is imprisoned in the castle, "till either time end
your days or Cynthia her displeasure". This is an ironic
reference to the pageant of 1582 and to the Castle of
Perfect Beauty which represented virginity and Elizabeth
I. The symbolism in the play is that Tellus, Elizabeth the
woman, has been imprisoned by Cynthia, Elizabeth the

monarch, and the "flower of beauty", Elizabeth the woman, will "wither in prison".

Eumenides, the private Earl of Oxford, says that for seven years he has kept secret his love for his sweet mistress and has not "nor once darest not, to name her for discontenting her". His sweet mistress is Semele, "She of all women the most froward (Latin 'vernilis'), and I of all creatures the most fond (Latin 'devia', foolish)". Eumenides is told that only a faithful lover can read the words at the bottom of a fountain. Eumenides says: "I plainly see the bottom, and there in white marble engraven these words: Ask one for all, and but one thing at all".

The words that Eumenides, the private Earl of Oxford, can see and which therefore prove that he is a faithful lover of Semele, "whose golden locks seem most curious when they seem most careless", were created from the motto of the Earl of Southampton: One for all, all for one. Therefore it is the Earl of Southampton who is the proof that the Earl of Oxford is a faithful lover of Elizabeth I.

Eumenides then sees these words: "When she, whose figure of all is the perfectest and neVer to be measured, always one, yet ('nihilominus') neVer the same, still ('nihilominus') inconstant ('devia') yet ('nihilominus') neVer waVering, shall come and kiss Endimion in his sleep, he shall then rise; else neVer". These lines were constructed from the repeating of neVer which was combined with the repeating of 'nihilominus' to create a motto pun. The line "always one, yet never the same" is a reworking of the line in sonnet 76: "Why write I still all one, ever the same", and the implication is that although Elizabeth I's motto was "Always the same" she was in actuality "never the same". The inclusion of the words "all" and "one" incorporates into these lines puns on the mottoes of the Earl of Oxford, Elizabeth I, and the Earl of Southampton, as in sonnet 76.

Eumenides then says: "There cometh over mine eyes either a dark mist, or upon the fountain a deep thickness, for I can perceive ('advertere', to perceive) nothing ('nihil')". For I can perceive de Vere.

The solution to the riddle is that a circle of all figures is the perfectest and that Cynthia of all circles is the most absolute. "Then who can it be but Cynthia, whose virtues being all divine, must needs bring things to pass that be miraculous". Cynthia will resolve the entanglements of Endimion, Eumenides, Tellus, and Semele; and because Cynthia is a symbolical representation of Elizabeth the monarch, it is Elizabeth the monarch who will resolve the entanglements of de Vere the public man, de Vere the private man, and Elizabeth the woman.

John Lyly would never have dared to write lines which could be interpreted as meaning that Elizabeth I was not the Virgin Queen. The Earl of Oxford however, being the Lord Great Chamberlain of England and coming from a family whose noble line was more ancient than Elizabeth's, would have dared to write the lines that could be interpreted in such a way.

In *The Woman in the Moon* de Vere makes it perfectly clear that the Latin grammar was irrelevant when he was constructing a pun. Pandora makes a prediction in Latin: "Utopiae Stesias Phoenici solvit amorem Numina caelorum dum pia praecipunt". When Stesias interprets this prediction he says: "If 'solvere amorem' signify 'to love' then means this prophecy good to Stesias". De Vere did not have Stesias repeat the actual words of the prediction "solvit amorem": he is releasing to, or from, love; but the present infinitive active 'solvere amorem': to release to, or from, love. He did this so that he could create a pun on his name by using the 'ver' word 'solvere'. In so doing de Vere is showing us how he constructed the puns; not just this pun, but all of the puns. He had in mind the present infinitive active form of a Latin verb even when the verb was in the third person, or any other number, tense, mood or voice.

Although the plays that have been attributed to John Lyly are quite short, they contain, in addition to the puns on de Vere's name, an average of eighteen puns on the Earl of Oxford's motto.

The name of Christopher Marlowe was chosen for the Earl of Oxford to hide behind because Marlowe had been well educated at Cambridge and also because he was dead when it was decided to attribute the plays to him.

William Shakspere was chosen because de Vere was probably known as Will or Willy to his literary and theatrical friends, from the Latin word 'avere' to wish, to will; because of the coat of arms of de Vere's second title of the Viscount Bulbeck, which shows a lion brandishing or shaking a broken spear; because Pallas, the goddess of poets and dramatists, was known as the spear shaker; and most importantly, because Shakspere could be conveniently hidden away in the distant town of Stratford-upon-Avon, three days journey from London.

Academic commentators believe that in his comedies Shakespeare was influenced by the plays of John Lyly, and that in his tragedies Shakespeare had been influenced by Christopher Marlowe. It is therefore not surprising that it is not only in the plays of 'Shakespeare' but also in the plays of 'Lyly' and 'Marlowe' that large numbers of puns can be found on the Earl of Oxford's name and motto. This indicates that all of the plays that have been attributed to 'Lyly' and 'Marlowe', as well as to 'Shakespeare', must have been written by the Earl of Oxford.

Edward de Vere had been robbed of his 'good name', and he knew that he would never be acknowledged as the true author of his plays during his lifetime. However, as his 'good name' was more important to him than all of the lands, estates, and properties which he had lost, he incorporated his name, and his motto, into the plays and poems that he was writing, in the hope that future generations would allow him the recognition denies during his lifetime.

V

Contemporary Plays

I had found an average of twenty-six puns on the Earl of Oxford's family motto in the 'Shakespeare' plays. Some of the longer plays like *Antony and Cleopatra, Othello* and *Hamlet* contain more than forty motto puns. In all of the 'Shakespeare', 'Lyly' and 'Marlowe' plays I had found an average of twenty-four puns on the Earl of Oxford's motto.

Despite being absolutely convinced that the Earl of Oxford had written all of the plays attributed to 'Shakespeare', 'Lyly', and 'Marlowe', I felt that I had to read and analyse all of the Elizabethan and Jacobean plays that I could find to see whether they contain large numbers of puns on the Earl of Oxford's motto. If all of these other plays were to contain an average of twenty-four puns on the Earl of Oxford's motto it would show that the puns which I had already found were merely coincidental.

Altogether I read more than eighty plays written between about 1570 and 1625, including the 'Shakespeare', 'Lyly', and 'Marlowe' plays.

In the plays that definitely were not written by the Earl of Oxford I found an average of four puns on the Earl of Oxford's motto. Although this figure is more than I had anticipated it is six times less than the average number that I had found in the plays which I believe were written by the Earl of Oxford. Such a disparity argues that the average of twenty-four motto puns found in the plays of 'Shakespeare', 'Lyly', and 'Marlowe', cannot be coincidental.

Whilst analysing the eighty or so plays I came to the conclusion that any play that contains more than about ten or twelve puns on the Earl of Oxford's motto must seriously be considered as having been written by the Earl of Oxford, whereas those plays which contain fewer than six or seven motto puns could not be so attributed. When I had finished the analysis I realized that all of the plays fall into one of two categories: those plays which contain fourteen or more motto puns, and those plays which contain seven or fewer.

Two of these other plays which I have analysed each contain twenty-five motto puns.

The first of these plays is *The Two Noble Kinsmen*, included in the Oxford Shakespeare's *The Complete Works of William Shakespeare* because the play was said to have been written by John Fletcher and William Shakespeare. The twenty-five motto puns that I have found in this play are evenly distributed throughout the play, and not confined to those sections which are supposed to have been written by Shakespeare. They occur irrespective of whether particular sections are thought to have been written by either Fletcher or Shakespeare. This suggests to me that the whole of *The Two Noble Kinsmen* was written by the Earl of Oxford, probably at two different periods in his life.

The second of these plays that contain twenty-five puns on the Earl of Oxford's motto is *The Spanish Tragedy*, usually attributed to Thomas Kyd. However, it was not until 1612 that Kyd was first suggested as having been the author of the play, and 1773 before his name first appeared on a publication of the play.

Commentators point to some similarities between *The Spanish Tragedy* and *Hamlet*.

In his Preface to Greene's *Menaphon*, Thomas Nashe wrote in 1589: "yet English Seneca read by candlelight yields many good sentences . . . . and if you entreat him fair in a frosty morning, he will afford you whole Hamlets, I should say handfuls of tragical speeches". Because of this reference to Hamlet in 1589, commentators believe that there must have been an early *Hamlet* play, and that 'Shakespeare' used this early play as a source for his *Hamlet*. Also, because Nashe refers to the "English Seneca", and because *The Spanish Tragedy* is said to be in the style of Seneca, the commentators say that the "English Seneca" must have been Thomas Kyd, and that it was therefore Kyd who wrote the early *Hamlet*.

As well as the twenty-five motto puns, *The Spanish Tragedy* contains the 'ver' word clusters and 'ver' word connections which can be found in the plays of 'Shakespeare', 'Lyly', and 'Marlowe'. Therefore it was the Earl of Oxford who almost certainly wrote *The Spanish Tragedy*, it was he who was the "English Seneca", and it was he who wrote the early *Hamlet*, sometime before 1589, probably rewriting it after Lord Burghley's death in 1598.

There is a third play that contains seventeen puns on the Earl of Oxford's motto, and which therefore must seriously be considered as having been written by Edward de Vere. Even today the author of this play is still unknown, although some commentators have said it is the "best of the apocryphal plays" and that it must have "a fair claim to admittance to the Shakespeare canon". The play is called *Arden of Faversham*.

More than half of the seventeen puns on the motto appear in scenes one and fourteen, which are the two longest scenes in the whole play. Although most of the play does not show the slightest resemblance to the way de Vere constructed his plays, whole episodes in these two scenes, particularly scene fourteen, were constructed from the repetition of two, three, four, or more 'ver' words, which were combined with 'nihil' or 'nihilominus'.

It therefore appears to me that *Arden of Faversham*

may be a very early play from about 1578 and that it was probably written by Edward de Vere before he started constructing his plays from puns on his name and motto. He may have made additions and amendments about ten years later, creating name and motto puns, with particular attention being given to scenes one and fourteen.

A play called *The historie of Error*, which may have been an early version of *The Comedy of Errors*, was performed at the court in January 1577, and a month later a play called *The historye of Titus and Gisippus*, which may have been an early version of *Titus Andronicus*, was also performed at court. These plays, like *Arden of Faversham* were probably written by the Earl of Oxford, who had started to write plays when he returned from his tour of Europe in 1576. By 1590 he had written and seen performed most of the plays subsequently attributed to Shakespeare.

During the last fourteen or fifteen years of his life the Earl of Oxford did not write more than ten new plays, but spent most of his time rewriting and amending those plays which he had written in the 1570s and 1580s, polishing them in the new style of writing which he had created with the 'Lyly' plays in the late 1570s and early 1580s so that they would shine as brightly as the 'Shakespeare' plays of the 1590s and 1600s.

The Earl of Oxford was the literary colossus of the Elizabethan period and, just as Shakespeare is said to have been influenced by Lyly and Marlowe, so I believe that well into the seventeenth century those writers who came after the Earl of Oxford were influenced by his style of writing. His influence on these other writers can be seen in the way that elements of his style of writing appear in their plays, although not in the same quantity or with the same amount of complexity.

Because of the frequent clustering and repeating of 'ver' words there are 50% more puns on the name of de Vere in a de Vere play than there are in a play of equal length written by Peele, Marston, Jonson, or Middleton. The use of translations of 'ver' words by these writers is really quite sparse when compared to their use in a de Vere play.

In a play written by de Vere there is an average of 24 motto puns, whereas in a play not written by de Vere there is an average of only four motto puns. Most of the motto puns in a de Vere play were constructed from complex multiple 'ver' word repeatings and clustering, whereas in a play not written by de Vere most of this average of four puns on the motto were constructed by simply using the 'ver' word twice; for example: 'ver' word, 'nihil' or 'nihilominus', 'ver' word.

This average of four can, I think, be equally divided between those puns written as a tribute to the Earl of Oxford, acknowledging him as the greatest writer of the age, and those puns which, because of their simplistic nature, which is rare in a de Vere play, must have been written subliminally because of the subconscious influence of his style of writing, just as A. L. Rowse suggests that Shakespeare was subconsciously influenced by Marlowe's style of writing.

An example of how hidden puns on de Vere's name and motto were used to acknowledge de Vere as the greatest dramatist of the age can be found in Edmund Spenser's poem *Tears of the Muses* which was written in 1590. Spenser asks:

> Where be the sweet delight of Learning's treasure
> That wont with comic sock to beautify
> The painted theatres, and fill with pleasure
> The listeners' eyes and ears with melody . . . ?

this is followed by:

> And he, the man (Latin 'vir') whom nature (Latin 'veritas') self had made
> To mock (Latin 'veri ludificatio', mockery) her self, and truth to imitate (Latin 'imitari veritatem'),

the Latin word 'veritas' means truth, but can also be

defined as nature or the truth of nature; the literal translation of 'imitari veritatem' is to imitate truth or nature. Therefore in these lines Spenser connected "nature" to "truth to imitate" with the Latin 'veritas' and 'imitari veritatem', which shows that he intended to use the Latin words. The lines continue:

> With kindly counter under mimic shade
> Our pleasant Willy, ah! is dead of late.

Spenser does not mean that Willy is dead, only that he has "withdrawn from the public". This is confirmed in the next stanza but one when Spenser writes that Willy

> Doth rather choose to sit in idle cell
> Than to himself to mockery ('veri ludificatio') to sell.

So in 1590 Spenser is saying that a great writer of the theatre who is known as Willy has "withdrawn from the public" because he does not want to subject himself to mockery.

The Latin phrase 'nihil agere' means to do nothing, to be at rest, to be idle; and therefore, although these lines are not as compact as if they had been written by Edward de Vere, they can be interpreted as having been constructed from the Latin words 'veritas', 'veri ludificatio', 'imitari veritatem', 'nihil agere', and 'veri ludificatio'; which is a motto pun. The hidden meaning of these lines is that the great writer of the theatre who was known as Willy was the Earl of Oxford.

Edward de Vere himself used these same Latin words as the basis of the great debate between Polixenes and Perdita in *The Winter's Tale*, interpreting 'veritas' as being simply nature, as did Spenser, but interpreting 'imitari veritatem' to be true to nature, of works of art, as being simply art, as has been noted previously.

The Shoemaker's Holiday was written in 1599 by Thomas Dekker and, in Act IV, Scene v, Dekker reworks the lines from *Henry VI Part Two* Act IV, Scene vi, as follows:

Lord Mayor: But art thou sure ('vero', to be sure) of this?

Firk: Am I sure ('vero') that Paul's steeple is a handful higher than London Stone? Or that the pissing conduit leaks nothing ('nihil') but pure Mother Bunch? Am I sure ('vero') I am lusty Firk?

In *Henry VI Part Two* 'Shakespeare' refers to the 'pissing conduit' because it could be interpreted as being flowing water and would therefore be the Latin 'fluvius'. He also refers to London Stone because Vere House, the London home of the de Vere family, was close by London Stone. Dekker reworked the reference to the pissing conduit and London Stone so that he could again connect de Vere to *Henry VI*. He reinforced this connection by constructing the lines from a pun on the Earl of Oxford's motto, the pun being 'vero, vero, nihil, vero'. Also, the Latin word 'vere' can be interpreted as meaning pure, although this translation is a fairly rare occurrence.

Dekker constructed these lines and created the pun on the Earl of Oxford's motto to identify Oxford as being the author of *Henry VI*. In so doing he was also paying a tribute to de Vere by acknowledging that the writer of *Henry VI* deserved to be recognized.

It was George Chapman who wrote the continuation of 'Marlowe's' unfinished narrative poem *Hero and Leander*, and it is Chapman's *Bussy D'Ambois* that is most like a de Vere play. Although there are three or four motto puns in this play with a complexity worthy of the Earl himself, the total number of motto puns in the play is less than a third of the average number of motto puns in a 'Shakespeare' play, and only about a sixth of the number that can be found in a long 'Shakespeare' play like *Othello*.

The most interesting lines in the play are probably those that are spoken by the ghost after Bussy D'Ambois has died; they are: "Farewell (Latin 'avere'), brave relic of a complete man ('vir'); Look (Spanish 'ver', to look) up and see (Spanish 'ver', to see) thy spirit made a star".

The repeating of the Spanish word 'ver' makes it clear that Chapman's intention was to construct these lines from puns on de Vere's name, and if we look up we see the pole star, the constant star, the true star that can be seen on the shield of Edward de Vere. Therefore Chapman was implying in these lines that it is Edward de Vere's spirit that is "made a star".

Commentators believe that *Bussy D'Ambois* was written in 1604. I believe that these lines of the ghost were probably added on to the end of the play after de Vere's death in June 1604, and that these lines, perhaps the whole play, were written as a tribute to him.

An average of four motto puns occur in the plays of Ben Jonson who, I believe, used the puns as a way of identifying some of his characters as being caricatures of Edward de Vere, the best drawn being in *The Alchemist* which Jonson wrote in 1610, six years after de Vere's death.

Oxford was one of the leading men of fashion in Elizabethan England and I therefore think that the character of Dapper is a caricature of him. Dapper has come to the alchemist hoping to receive a familiar spirit for his gambling at horses. As has been noted previously the Latin 'veredus' means a swift horse, and when referring to de Vere the horses can stand as a metaphor for his plays. Therefore the analogy is that de Vere hopes to receive some good fortune with his plays.

We are told that Dapper is a clerk, a court writer, and in Act I, Scene ii he says: "By this hand of flesh, would it might never write good court hand more . . . .". In the analogy Dapper's writing at the law court can be taken as meaning de Vere's writing of plays for the court of Elizabeth. We are also told that Dapper "consorts with the small poets of the time", meaning that he aspires to be a small poet, whereas Jonson's intention was to imply that de Vere condescended to consort with the small poets of the time. Dapper "knows the law, and writes you six fair hands", which again applies to court writing but which implies that de Vere knew six languages, which were probably English, Latin, Greek, French, Italian, and Spanish. Dapper can also "Court his mistress out of Ovid", which would also apply to "Shakespeare". The character of Subtle says: "He's o' the only best complexion, the Queen of Faery loves", which is followed by: "The Doctor swears that you are – Allied to the Queen of Faery". It is only if the Queen of Faery "takes a fancy" to Dapper that Dapper will receive his good fortune. The Queen of Faery, as in Spenser's *The Faerie Queene*, represents Elizabeth I.

In Act III, Scene iv we are told that Dapper is a young gentleman who was "born to nothing, forty marks a year, which I count nothing". Jonson would have known that by 1590 de Vere had sold all of his lands and estates, his inheritance, his fortune. He would also have known the significance of "nothing" as an abbreviation of de Vere's motto and of his life.

We are told that when Dapper receives the familiar spirit: "They will set him upmost, at the groom porter's, all the Christmas! And for the whole year through, at every place, where there is play, present him with the chair; the best attendance, the best drink (French 'prendre un verre', to take a drink), sometimes two glasses ('verre') of canary, and pay nothing ('nihil') . . . . and those that drink ('prendre un verre') to no mouth else, will drink ('prendre un verre') to his, as being the goodly, president mouth of all the board.". These lines, although they are a little diffused, were constructed from 'prendre un verre', 'verre', 'nihil', and then a few lines later 'prendre un verre', 'prendre un verre'; which, being a motto pun, alludes to de Vere, the Lord Great Chamberlain, being "upmost" at the "groom porter's", which was the office of the Lord Chamberlain who superintended play at cards and dice. In the analogy the metaphor of gambling at the horses has been extended to include cards and dice and therefore "where there is play" represents the theatre rather than play at a gaming table. It is in the theatre where de Vere is presented with the chair, the place of honour.

In Scene v Subtle says: "the Faery Queen dispenses, by me, this robe, the petticoat of Fortune; which that he straight put on, she doth importune. And though to Fortune near be her petticoat, yet nearer is her smock, the Queen doth note". If the Italian word 'avere' is interpreted as meaning "Fortune" these lines form the motto pun 'avere, avere, nihilominus', even though this form, with 'nihilominus' coming after the 'ver' words, is very rare in a de Vere play.

Dapper is blindfolded with a piece of rag, which is supposed to be part of the Queen of Faery's smock. Subtle then says: "And trusting until her to make his state, He'll throw away all worldly pelf about him", which, of course, is exactly what the Earl of Oxford did after he had sold his lands and estates: he trusted Elizabeth to make his state and spent all the money which he received from her. Dapper is then told that: "her Grace will send her faeries here to search you . . . . If they find that you conceal a mite, you are undone"; to which Dapper replies:

	Truly (Latin 'vero'), there's all.
Face:	All what?
Dapper:	My money, truly ('vero').
Face:	Keep nothing ('nihil') that is transitory about you.

These lines were constructed from the words 'vero', 'vero', nihil', which is a motto pun, although again in a form very rarely used by de Vere, the 'nihil' coming after the 'ver' word, which is used only twice.

Face, Subtle and Dol then pinch Dapper, who believes that he is being pinched by fairies. This episode is a lampoon of Falstaff believing that he is being pinched by fairies in *The Merry Wives of Windsor*, which is itself a lampoon of Corsites actually being pinched by fairies in *Endimion*. By equating Dapper with Falstaff and Corsites Jonson was connecting his caricature of de Vere with

'Shakespeare' and 'Lyly', which possibly implies that the Earl of Oxford wrote *The Merry Wives of Windsor* and *Endimion*.

At this point Subtle receives a visit from Sir Epicure Mammon and it is decided that Dapper should be gagged and bestowed in 'the privy', which Subtle says is "Fortune's privy lodgings". During the last fourteen or fifteen years of his life the impoverished de Vere lived the life of a private gentleman having withdrawn from public affairs. This was de Vere's "privy lodgings", the consequence of his good fortune from Elizabeth I. He was also made "tongue tied by authority", in other words gagged.

In Act V we are told that the gingerbread gag has melted and Subtle says to Dapper: "your aunt her Grace, will give you audience presently, on my suit . . . . that you did not eat your gag in contempt of her Highness". To which Dapper replies: "Not I, in troth (Latin 'vero' in truth)". De Vere continued to write his plays, although he still could not reveal himself. Dol Common then disguises herself as the Queen of Faery and says to Dapper: "Much nephew, shalt thou win, much shalt thou spend, much shalt thou give away, much shalt thou lend", and Subtle says: "Much indeed (Latin 'vere')".

The familiar or fly is then given to Dapper and Subtle says: "Your fly will learn you all games . . . . Your Grace will command him no more duties?" To which Dol replies: "No". De Vere did not perform any service or duties for queen or country during the whole of his life. Jonson is therefore saying that Elizabeth gave the Earl of Oxford a pension of one thousand pounds a year, which is equated by Jonson in this lampoon as the fly, familiar, or good luck charm which is given to Dapper, and that she allowed him to spend his life at games, a symbolism for frivolities like the theatre and literary activities.

In return for being given the spirit of gaming, Dapper has to give up his forty marks a year, and he says that he'll give his court writings to the Queen of Faery. Jonson is symbolically saying that in return for being given a pension of one thousand pounds per year the Earl of

Oxford gave his court writings, his theatrical and literary manuscripts, to Elizabeth I.

Although Jonson may not have been a particularly close friend of the Earl of Oxford he was a literary colleague who probably knew de Vere quite well. It would therefore not be surprising if the caricature of de Vere had suggested itself to Jonson as he remembered conversations he had had with de Vere.

In the poem that he dedicated "To the memory of my beloved, The Author, Master William Shakespeare", in the First Folio of *Comedies, Histories, and Tragedies*, published in 1623, Jonson wrote:

> Look how the father's face
> Lives in his issue, even so the race
> Of Shakespeare's mind and manners brightly shines
> In his well turned and true filed lines,
> In each of which he seems to shake a lance,
> As brandished at the eyes of ignorance.

These lines of course refer to the patron of dramatists and poets Pallas, who was born out of the brow of Zeus shaking a lance. They also refer to de Vere's Viscount Bulbeck coat of arms which shows a lion shaking or brandishing a broken spear or lance to signify his courage. And they recall the words of Gabriel Harvey who said that the Earl of Oxford had the countenance of one who shakes spears! Jonson then calls "Shakespeare": "Sweet swan of Avon", and of course de Vere did have a house on the Avon, Bilton Manor at Rugby, where he probably spent quite a lot of his time during the last fourteen or fifteen years of his life. And towards the end of the poem Jonson wrote: "Shine forth, thou star of poets", which, as we have seen, could refer to the de Vere star, the true star on the shield of the Earls of Oxford, which would connect with the "true filed lines" of "Shakespeare".

Some of the most interesting lines in the poem however are these:

For if I thought my judgement were of years,
I should commit thee surely with thy peers,
And tell how far thou didst our Lyly outshine,
Or sporting Kyd, or Marlowe's mighty line.

Why did Jonson not say that "Shakespeare" had outshone some of the dramatists who were alive at the time, like Middleton, Ford, Webster, or even Jonson himself? Probably because no matter how great "Shakespeare" had been it would have been a slight to the living writers. So why did Jonson not mention Sidney, or Spenser? Why did Jonson single out Lyly, Kyd, and Marlowe from the vast array of Elizabethan and Jacobean writers who had been outshone by "Shakespeare"? Was it purely coincidence? I think not. Jonson had deliberately chosen those very same dramatists whose plays, along with those of "Shakespeare", contain an average of twenty-four puns on the motto of the Earl of Oxford. Jonson chose Lyly, Kyd, and Marlowe because he knew that it would not be a slight to them to have been outshone by "Shakespeare", because he knew that the plays of "Lyly", "Kyd", and "Marlowe" were the early plays of "Shakespeare", and that all of the plays attributed to "Lyly", "Kyd", "Marlowe", and "Shakespeare" had been written by Edward de Vere.

In the eighty-one lines of the poem which Ben Jonson dedicated to the memory of William Shakespeare, there are seventy-odd puns on the Earl of Oxford's name, and two double motto puns, the most interesting of which can be found in these lines:

"Nature ('veritas') herself was proud of his designs,
And joyed to wear the dressing of his lines ('versus', a line, especially of poetry),
Which were so richly spun, and woven so fit,
As since she will vouchsafe no other wit.
The merry Greek, tart Aristophanes,
Neat Terence, witty Plautus, now not please,

But antiquated and deserted lie
As they were not of nature's ('veritas') family.
Yet ('nihilominus') must I not give nature ('veritas') all; thy art ('imitari veritatem'),
My gentle Shakespeare, must enjoy a part.
For though the poet's ('versificator', a verse-maker) matter nature ('veritas') be,
His art ('imitari veritatem') doth give the fashion; and that he
Who casts to write a living line ('versus') must sweat –
Such as thine are – and strike the second heat
Upon the muses' anvil, turn ('vertere') the same,
And himself with it that he thinks ('versare', to think over) to frame . . . .

As in the great debate between Polixenes and Perdita in *The Winter's Tale*, these lines were constructed from the interpretation of the Latin 'veritas' as being simply nature, and 'imitari veritatem' as being simply art. Derivations of the Latin 'vertere', in the form of 'versus', 'versare', and 'versificator' were also connected. When combined with the 'nihilominus' these lines form a pun on the Earl of Oxford's motto.

Ben Jonson had constructed the poem in exactly the same way, the same Euphuistic style, as those poems and plays which had been written by the Earl of Oxford. Ben Jonson's memorial poem to Shakespeare is the complete and ultimate tribute to Edward de Vere.

In 1623 the implication of Ben Jonson's poem to the memory of William Shakespeare, for those who could see, would have been obvious. It was only those who could not see who accepted the deception that "Shakespeare" was the man from Stratford-upon-Avon. And today it is only those who cannot see, or will not see, who are convinced that "Shakespeare" was the man from Stratford-upon-Avon.

Of course only a relatively small number of his contemporaries would have known that Oxford had written the plays. These would have included his family, his literary and theatrical friends, the nobility at the courts of Elizabeth I and James I, and possibly some of the educated professions.

Gradually, with each succeeding generation, the secret of the Earl of Oxford's hidden wit became known to fewer and fewer people; and with the closing of the theatres, the period of the Protectorate, and the Civil War, it was forgotten. As his hidden wit was gradually forgotten, so the Earl of Oxford was gradually forgotten.

With the discovery of the hidden wit in the works that have been attributed to 'Lyly', 'Kyd', 'Marlowe', and 'Shakespeare', there can now be no doubt that the recognition which the Earl of Oxford deserves is long overdue.

One of the reasons why no one in the past has found the hidden wit in the works of Shakespeare is because the Earl of Oxford did not always use the conventional translations of foreign words. Therefore, if we rigidly adhere to traditional translations, quite a lot of this hidden wit cannot be found. We have to try to enter the creative mind of de Vere so that we can understand how he dressed or interpreted some of the translations in new ways.

There are more than fifty thousand puns on the name of de Vere in the Shakespeare plays. Some of them are absolutely precise, some of them are a little insubstantial. Some of them are an exact translation of a word, and some of them are de Vere's rather loose interpretation of a word. I am not a professional linguist, but the only ability necessary is to find the appropriate entries in the appropriate language dictionary.

I have found all of the 'ver' words and phrases, and their definitions, in the following reference books:

Collins-Robert French Dictionary. 2nd ed. Collins, London, 1987.

Collins-Sansoni Italian Dictionary. 3rd ed. Sansoni, Firenze, 1988.

Collins Spanish Concise Dictionary. Collins, London, 1985.

Lewis, Charlton T. *and* Short, Charles. *A Latin Dictionary.* Clarendon Press, Oxford, 1933.

Oxford English Dictionary.

Rebora, Piero. *Italian-English Dictionary.* 7th ed. Cassell, London, 1967.

Simpson, D. P. *Latin Dictionary.* 5th ed. Cassell, London, 1987.

✳   ✳   ✳

Select Bibliography

Allen, Percy. *The Case for Edward de Vere, 17th Earl of Oxford as Shakespeare.* Cecil Palmer, London, 1930.

Allen, Percy. *The Life Story of Edward de Vere as "William Shakespeare".* Cecil Palmer, London, 1932.

Allen, Percy. *Anne Cecil, Elizabeth & Oxford.* Archer, London, 1934. 1948. 3rd ed. by Ruth Loyd Miller. Minos Publishing Co., P.O. Box 1309, Jennings, LA 70546, 1975.

Allen, Percy. *The Oxford-Shakespeare case corroborated.* Cecil Palmer, London, 1931.

American Shakespeare Fellowship. *Newsletter,* 1939-48.

Amphlett, Hilda. *Who Was Shakespeare?* Heinemann, London, 1955. Reissued by A.M.S. Press, New York, 1972.

Anderson, Verily. *The De Veres of Castle Hedingham.* Terence Dalton, Lavenham, 1993.

Arden of Faversham. Ernest Benn, London, 1982.

Baldwin, T. W. *Shakspere's Small Latine and Lesse Greek.* U. of Illinois P., Urbana, 1944.

Beaumont, Francis. *The Knight of the Burning Pestle.* Ernest Benn, London, 1969.

Bénézet, Louis P. *Shakspere, Shakespeare and de Vere.* Granite State Press, Manchester, NH, 1937.

Boas, Frederick S. *Christopher Marlowe.* Clarendon Press, Oxford, 1940.

Bradbrook, M. C. *The Artist and Society in Shakespeare's England.* Harvester Press, Hassocks, 1982.

Bullough, Geoffrey. *Narrative and Dramatic Sources of Shakespeare.* Routledge, London, 1957.

Cairncross, Alfred S. *The Problem of Hamlet: a Solution.* Macmillan, London, 1936.

Cercignani, Fausto. *Shakespeare's Works and Elizabethan Pronunciation.* Oxford U.P., Oxford, 1981.

Challinor, A. M. *The Alternative Shakespeare: a Modern Introduction.* Book Guild, Lewes, 1996.
The pseudonym conceals the name of the Oxfordian Arthur Maltby.

Chapman, George. *Bussy D'Ambois.* Ernest Benn, London, 1965.

Churchill, R. C. *Shakespeare and his Betters.* Reinhardt, London, 1958.
A Stratfordian summarises the case for and against each claimant, basing his case against Oxford (like Wilson, below) on objections to shifting the dates of some plays back.

Clark, Eva Turner. *Hidden Allusions in Shakespeare's Plays.* 3rd ed. by Ruth Loyd Miller. Minos Publishing, P.O. Box 1309, Jennings, LA 70546, 1974.

De Vere Society *Newsletter.* Quarterly journal. The De Vere Society, 8 Western Road, Henley-on-Thames, RG9 1JL.
(Membership of the Society entitles the member to receive also the quarterly Shakespeare Oxford Society *Newsletter*, q.v.)

Dekker, Thomas. *The Shoemaker's Holiday.* A. & C. Black, London, 1986.

Dent, R. W. *Shakespeare's Proverbial Language.* U. of California P., Berkeley, 1981.

Detobel, Robert. *Oxford, Lyly, Nashe and Greene vs Harvey.* The De Vere Society, 8 Western Road, Henley-on-Thames, RG9 1JL, 1997.
Argues that de Vere covertly participated in a war of pamphlets against Gabriel Harvey.

Dictionary of National Biography. Ed. by Leslie Stephen and Sidney Lee. Smith, Elder, London, 1908.
Sidney Lee wrote the entries for both Shakespeare and the Earl of Oxford, without making any connection.

Douglas, Montagu. *Lord Oxford and the Shakespeare Group.* Alden Press, London, 1952.
The third ed. of a book published previously as *Lord Oxford as Shakespeare* (1931) and *Lord Oxford was Shakespeare* (1934). Argues that de Vere collaborated with his son-in-law the Earl of Derby, his cousin Francis Bacon, and certain professional dramatists.

Dunlop, Ian. *Palaces and Progresses of Elizabeth I.* Cape, London, 1962.

Dusinberre, Juliet. *Shakespeare and the Nature of Women.* Macmillan, London, 1979.

Edwards, Philip. *Shakespeare: A Writer's Progress.* Oxford U.P., Oxford, 1987.

Elizabethan Review. Journal ed. and pub. by Gary B. Goldstein, 123-60 83rd Ave., Kew Gardens, N.Y. 11415.

English Shakespeare Fellowship. *Newsletter,* 1943-58.

Falconer, A. F. *Shakespeare and the Sea.* Constable, London, 1964.

Fiehler, Rudolf. *The Strange Case of Sir John Oldcastle*. American Press, 1965.

Field, Andrew. *The Lost Chronicle of Edward de Vere*. Viking, London, 1990.

Ford, John. *'Tis Pity She's a Whore*. A. & C. Black, London, 1990.

Forrest, H. T. S. *The Original Venus and Adonis*. Bodley Head, London, 1930.

Fowler, William Plumer. *Shakespeare Revealed in Oxford's Letters*. P. E. Randall, Portsmouth, N.H., 1986.
Linguistic and literary parallels between de Vere's extant letters and Shakespeare's works.

Fox, Levi. *The Shakespeare Handbook*. Bodley Head, London, 1987.

Fraser, Russell. *The War against Poetry*. Princeton U.P., Princeton, N.J., 1970.
Discusses the threat posed to the commercial and clerical elite in Elizabethan England by the wave of popularity of drama and poetry.

Frisbee, George. *Edward de Vere: a Great Elizabethan*. Cecil Palmer, London, 1931.

Gibson, H. N. *The Shakespeare Claimants*. Methuen, London, 1962.
A Stratfordian defence against Bacon, Derby, Marlowe and Oxford.

Golding, Louis Thorn. *An Elizabethan Portrait: Arthur Golding*. R. D. Smith, New York, 1937.

Greenwood, G. George. *Is There a Shakespeare Problem?* Bodley Head, London, 1916.
A response to critics of his earlier book, below.

Greenwood, G. George. *The Shakespeare Problem Restated*. Bodley Head, London, 1908.
The British M.P. and lawyer produces a devastating case against the possibility of Will Shakspere's having written the works attributed to Shakespeare, though he offers no alternative.

Gregory, Tappan, *ed. Shakespeare Cross-Examination*. Chicago, 1961.
Reprints articles and letters from the *American Bar Association Journal*. For an answer to the Oxfordian ideas expressed here, see Martin, below.

Halliday, F. E. *The Cult of Shakespeare*. Duckworth, London, 1957.

Hamilton, Charles. *In Search of Shakespeare: Life and Handwriting*. Robert Hale, London, 1986.

Harvey, Gabriel. *Works*. Collected and with introd. and notes by Alexander Grosart. Privately printed, London, 1884.
See under Detobel above.

Heywood, Thomas. *A Woman Killed with Kindness*. A. & C. Black, London, 1985.

Hoffman, Calvin. *The Murder of the Man Who Was Shakespeare*. J. Messner, New York, 1955.
A Marlovian approach.

Holland, Hubert H. *Shakespeare, Oxford and Elizabethan Times*. Archer, London, 1933.

Holland, Hubert H. *Shakespeare Through Oxford Glasses*. Cecil Palmer, London, 1923.

Holmes, Martin. *Shakespeare and Burbage*. Phillimore, Chichester, 1978.

Honigman, E. A. J. *Shakespeare's Impact on his Contemporaries*. Macmillan, London, 1982.

Hope, Warren *and* Holston, Kim. *The Shakespeare Controversy: an Analysis of the Claimants to Authorship and their Champions and Detractors*. McFarland, Jefferson, NC, 1992.
A brief text, but valuable for its annotated bibliography in chronological order.

Hotson, Leslie. *Mr. W. H.* Hart-Davis, London, 1984.

Hughes, Ted. *Shakespeare and the Goddess of Complete Being*. Faber, London, 1992.

Hume, Martin. *The Great Lord Burghley*. Eveleigh Nash, London, 1908.

Huston, Craig. *The Shakespeare Authorship Question: Evidence for Edward de Vere, 17th Earl of Oxford*. Dorrance, Philadelphia, 1971.

Johnson, Paul. *Elizabeth I: a Study In Power And Intellect*. Weidenfeld and Nicolson, London, 1974.

Jonson, Ben. *Works*. Ed. by C. H. Herford and P. and E. Simpson. Clarendon Press, Oxford, 1947.

Kay, Dennis. *Shakespeare: his Life, Work and Era*. Sidgwick and Jackson, London, 1992.

Knight, G. Wilson. *The Imperial Theme*. Methuen, London, 1985.

Krass, Iris *and* Dams, Christopher H. *Discovering the True Shake-spear, William Shakspere or Edward de Vere?* The De Vere Society, 8 Western Road, Henley-on-Thames, RG9 1JL, 1994.
A pamphlet summarising the Oxfordian position.

Kyd, Thomas. *The Spanish Tragedy*. A. & C. Black, London, 1989.

Levi, Peter. *The Life and Times Of William Shakespeare*. Macmillan, London, 1988.

Looney, J. Thomas. *"Shakespeare" Identified in Edward de Vere, the 17th Earl of Oxford*. Cecil Palmer, London, 1920. 2nd ed. Foreword by William McFee. Duell, Sloan and Pearce, New York, 1949. 3rd ed. by Ruth Loyd Miller. Minos Publishing Co., P.O. Box 1309, Jennings, LA 70546, 1975.
Ruth Loyd Miller's two-volume set incorporates Looney's original text and *The Poems of Edward de Vere, Seventeenth Earl of Oxford*, with Looney's original introduction and notes, the whole comprising pp. 537-644 in her Vol. I. Vol. II, entitled *Oxfordian Vistas* (Minos Publishing Co., P.O. Box 1309, Jennings, LA 70546), is a compilation of 24 articles on Oxford, the Shakespeare authorship question, and the Elizabethan background, together with a map and directory of de Vere's London, and a bibliography of the writings of Charles Wisner Barrell, who edited the Shakespeare Fellowship *Newsletter* and *Quarterly* from 1940-7.

Lyly, John. *The Plays of John Lyly*. Ed. by Carter A. Daniel. Associated U.P., London and Toronto, 1988.

Majendie, Severne A. A. *Some Account of the Family of de Vere*. 1904.

Marlowe, Christopher. *The Complete Plays*. Ed. by J. B. Steane. Penguin, London, 1969.

Marlowe, Christopher. *The Complete Poems and Translations.* Ed. by Stephen Orgel. Penguin, London, 1971.

Marston, John. *The Malcontent.* Ernest Benn, London, 1967.

Martin, Milward W. *Was Shakespeare Shakespeare? A Lawyer Reviews the Evidence.* Cooper Square, New York, 1965.
A Stratfordian reply to Gregory, above.

Matus, Irvin. *Shakespeare: the Facts.* Continuum, New York, 1994.
A Stratfordian reply to Oxfordian arguments.

Meres, Francis. *Palladis Tamia.* London, 1599.

Michell, J. *Who wrote Shakespeare?* Thames and Hudson, London, 1996.

Middleton, Thomas. *Five Plays.* Penguin, London, 1988.

Nashe, Thomas. *Complete Works.* Ed. by R. B. McKerrow. 5 vols. Basil Blackwell, Oxford, 1958.

Neilson, W. A. ed. *The Chief Elizabeth Dramatists excluding Shakespeare.* Harrap, London, 1911.

Nichols, J. G. *The Poetry of Sir Philip Sidney.* Liverpool U.P., Liverpool, 1974.

Nichols, John. *Progresses and Public Processions of Queen Elizabeth.* 3 vols. J. Nichols, London, 1823.

Ogburn, Charlton, *Jr. The Mysterious William Shakespeare.* Dodd, Mead, New York, 1984. 2nd ed. EPM Publications, McLean, VA 22101, 1992.
The one indispensable book repudiating the Stratford case and coming by forensic argument down to the one candidate who fits all the requirements: Edward de Vere. The notes are detailed, the chronology exemplary, and the bibliography comprehensive.

Ogburn, Dorothy *and* Ogburn, Charlton, *Jr. Shake-speare: The Man Behind the Name.* William Morrow, New York, 1962.
An Oxfordian comparison between Oxford and Shakspere as claimants to the authorship.

Ogburn, Dorothy *and* Ogburn, Charlton, *Sr. This Star of England.* Coward-McCann, New York, 1952.
A highly detailed biography of de Vere, indicating parallels with the works of Shakespeare.

PBS-TV. *The Shakespeare Mystery.* Broadcast first on 18 April 1989. Available on cassette no. 1-800-328-PBS 1.
The Stratfordian case is put by Samuel Schoenbaum and A. L. Rowse and others, while the Oxfordian case is stated by Charlton Ogburn, Jr., Lord Burford and J. Enoch Powell.

Peele, George. *The Old Wife's Tale* from *Three Sixteenth-Century Comedies.* Ed. by Charles W. Whitworth. Ernest Benn, London, 1984.

Phillips, G. *Lord Burghley in Shakespeare.* Thornton Butterworth, London, 1936.

Phillips, G. *The Tragic Story of "Shakespeare" disclosed in the Sonnets, and the Life of Edward de Vere, 17th Earl of Oxford.* Cecil Palmer, London, 1932.

Phillips, Graham *and* Keatman, Martin. *The Shakespeare Conspiracy.* Arrow Books, London, 1995.

Pollard, A. W. *Shakespeare's Fight with the Pirates*. Moring, London, 1917.
Pollard's analysis of Elizabethan literary piracy explains how the system of patronage retarded the development of professional authorship "by so lowering the status of authors . . . that no one with any pretensions to rank or fashion could take money for his writings. To escape any imputation of doing so, fashionable authors avoided print altogether, and circulated their writings among their friends in manuscript".

Pollard, A. W. *et al. Shakespeare's Hand in "Sir Thomas More"*. Cambridge U.P., Cambridge, 1923.

Puttenham, George. *The Arte of English Poesie* (1589), *Ancient Critical Essays*. Ed. by Joseph Haslewood. Robert Triphook, London, 1811.
For a discussion of the authorship of this text, see Ward, 'The Authorship . . .', below.

Quennell, P. *and* Quennell, J. H. *Who's Who in Shakespeare*. Chancellor Press, London, 1973.

Read, Conyers. *Lord Burghley & Queen Elizabeth*. Cape, London, 1960.

Rendall, Gerald H. *Personal Clues in Shakespeare's Poems and Sonnets*. Bodley Head, London, 1934.

Rendall, Gerald H. *Shakespeare: handwriting and spelling*. Cecil Palmer, London, 1931.
Concludes that the autograph manuscripts, from which the Quarto text was constructed, possessed the characteristics, and many of the individual peculiarities, of de Vere's script and spelling, and that his epistolary manner, in vocabulary, sentiments, and turns of speech, shows marked affinities with those in the Shakespearean sonnets.

Rendall, Gerald H. *Shakespeare's Sonnets and Edward de Vere*. John Murray, London, 1930.

Rowse, A. L. *Christopher Marlowe*. Macmillan, London, 1964.

Rowse, A. L. *William Shakespeare: A Biography*. Macmillan, London, 1963.
A vigorous Stratfordian account, rich in supposition.

Rubinstein, F. *A Dictionary of Shakespeare's Sexual Puns and their Significance*. Macmillan, London, 1984.

Salgado, Gamini. *ed. Eyewitnesses of Shakespeare Performances, 1590-1890*. Sussex U.P., Falmer, 1975.

Sams, Eric. *ed. Shakespeare's Lost Play, "Edmund Ironside"*. Fourth Estate, London, 1985.

Schoenbaum, Samuel. *William Shakespeare: a Documentary Life*. Oxford U.P., Oxford, 1975.
A Stratfordian view, abridged, revised and with a new postscript in 1987.

Schoenbaum, Samuel. *Shakespeare's Lives*. New ed. Oxford U.P., Oxford, 1991.
An account of the scholarship devoted to the Stratfordian, with a section on other claimants.

Sears, Elisabeth. *Shakespeare and the Tudor Rose*. Consolidated Press, Seattle, 1990.
Discusses the theory that the 3rd Earl of Southampton was the son of Elizabeth I and Edward de Vere.

Shakespeare, William. *The Complete Works*. The Cambridge text established by John Dover Wilson. Cambridge U.P., Cambridge, 1987.

Shakespeare, William. *The Complete Works*. Ed. by Stanley Wells and Gary Taylor. Clarendon Press, Oxford, 1988.

Shakespearean Authorship Review, 1959-74.

Shakespeare Oxford Society *Newsletter.* Quarterly journal. The Shakespeare Oxford Society, P.O. Box 263, Somerville, MA 02143.

Shakespeare Survey. Annual volumes from vol. I. Cambridge U.P., Cambridge, 1948-.

Sheavyn, Phoebe A. B. *The Literary Profession in the Elizabethan Age.* Manchester U.P., Manchester, 1967.
Her list of writers of aristocratic birth who could not publish under their own names includes de Vere, Dyer, Fletcher, Fulke Greville, Herbert, Hume, Raleigh, Sackville, Sidney and Wotton.

Shirley, F. A. *Swearing and Perjury in Shakespeare's Plays.* Allen & Unwin, London, 1979.

Speaight, Robert. *Shakespeare on the Stage.* Collins, London, 1973.
Especially valuable for its illustrations of costumes and sets in many ages and many countries.

Spenser, Edmund. *The Faerie Queene.* Ed. by Thomas P. Roche. Penguin, London, 1978.

Spevack, M. *The Harvard Concordance to Shakespeare.* Olms, Hildesheim, 1973.

Stopes, Charlotte C. *The Life of Henry, Third Earl of Southampton, Shakespeare's Patron.* Cambridge U.P., Cambridge, 1922.
Her seven-year search for a connection between Wriothesley and the Stratford man failed, and she openly confessed her time wasted.

Stritmatter, Roger. *The Quintessence of Dust.* Privately printed, 1992.
The Geneva bible bound with the arms of Edward de Vere is in the Folger Shakespeare Library is considered the Bible he is recorded to have bought at the age of nineteen. Of its thousand-plus annotations in manuscript, Stritmatter has identified at least 250-odd as being echoed in the plays of Shakespeare and/or in the extant letters of de Vere.

Taylor, Gary. *Reinventing Shakespeare.* Weidenfeld & Nicolson, London, 1989.
A Stratfordian account of how the reputation of Shakespeare developed over the centuries.

Theobald, Bertram G. *Enter Francis Bacon.* Cecil Palmer, London, 1932.
With a useful bibliography of 38 items. Bacon was a cousin of Robert Cecil, and so a cousin of Oxford by marriage.

Theobald, Bertram G. *Exit Shakspere.* Cecil Palmer, London, 1931.
A Baconian cites 25 reasons why the Stratford man is disqualified from being considered the true author.

Tillyard, E. M. W. *The Elizabethan World Picture.* Chatto & Windus, London, 1960.

Tillyard, E. M. W. *Shakespeare's Last Plays.* Chatto & Windus, London, 1964.

Tillyard, E. M. W. *Shakespeare's Problem Plays.* Chatto & Windus, London, 1951.

Twain, Mark. *Is Shakespeare Dead?* Harper, New York, 1909.
A satirical attack on the idea that Will Shakspere could have written the works attributed to Shakespeare.

Ure, Peter. *Elizabethan and Jacobean Drama.* Liverpool U.P., Liverpool, 1974.

Wadsworth, Frank W. *The Poacher from Stratford.* U. of California P., Berkeley, 1958.
A Stratfordian refutes the Baconian theory, and rejects Oxfordian claims without analysis.

Wait, R. J. C. *The Background to Shakespeare's Sonnets.* Chatto & Windus, London, 1972.

Ward, Bernard M. *The Authorship of "The Arte of English Poesie": a Suggestion.* The De Vere Society, 8 Western Road, Henley-on-Thames, RG9 1JL, 1996.
Reprinted from *Review of English Studies* (1925), this paper rejects the attribution to Puttenham, proposing instead the name of John, Lord Lumley, a fellow-courtier and friend of de Vere.

Ward, Bernard M. *ed. A Hundreth Sundrie Flowres,* 1573. From the original ed. Etchells & Macdonald, London, 1926. 2nd ed. by Ruth Loyd Miller. Minos Publishing Co., P.O. Box 1309, Jennings, LA 70546, 1975.
This anthology, long believed to be by George Gascoigne, was identified by Ward as the first Elizabethan poetical anthology. He identified the editor-poet as Oxford, whose posy 'Meritum petere, grave' appeared on the title-page of 1573.

Ward, Bernard M. *The Seventeenth Earl of Oxford (1550-1604), from Contemporary Documents.* John Murray, London, 1928. 2nd ed. by Ruth Loyd Miller. Minos Publishing Co., P.O. Box 1309, Jennings, LA 70546, 1975.
The classic documentary biography.

Webbe, Edward. *The Travels of Edward Webbe.* 1590.

Webster, John. *The Duchess Of Malfi and Other Plays.* Oxford U.P., Oxford, 1996.

Whalen, Richard F. *Shakespeare – who was he? The Oxford challenge to the Bard of Avon.* Praeger, 88 Post Road West, Westport, CT 06881, 1994.
The President of the Shakespeare Oxford Society's summary of the cases against Shakspere and for Oxford. His appendices cover 'Records of Will Shakspere's Theatre Activities' (there are no theatre records of him at all); the controversy about who wrote Greene's *Groatsworth of Wit* and its relevance to Shakspere; Jonson's reference in a notebook to Shakespeare, covered elsewhere at great length by Alden Brooks in his *This Side of Shakespeare* (Vantage, New York, 1964); and the Bénézet Test, devised to discover whether readers can tell the difference between lines of poetry written by de Vere before the age of 26 when interspersed in lines from the poems of Shakespeare.

Wilson, Ian. *Shakespeare: The Evidence.* Headline, London, 1993.

Index

Cambridge University
(St John's College), 4
(Trinity College), 13
Cardanus, Hieronymus
(Girolamo Cardano,
Jerôme Cardan), 7-8
Carey, *Sir* Henry. *See*
Hunsdon
Castiglione, Baldassare, 7,
13, 79
Cathay Company, 12-13
Cecil, Anne. *See* Oxford
Cecil, *Sir* Robert. *See*
Salisbury
Cecil, William. *See*
Burghley
Chapman, George, 121-2
Claudio (de Vere; in
Measure for Measure),
35
Cloten, 38
Cobham, *Lord* John, 24
Comedy of Errors, The, 35,
55, 118
Commedia dell' Arte, 10
Coriolanus, 83
Cornwall, 9-10
Corsites, 124
Craig, Hardin, 7
Cymbeline, 38, 56, 83
Cynthia (Elizabeth I),
111-3

Dapper (de Vere), 122-6
Dark Lady of the Sonnets,
16
dating the plays, 81-5
de Vere. *See* Oxford

Dekker, Thomas, 120-1
Derby, Elizabeth de Vere,
Countess of, 9, 17, 24
Derby, Ferdinando, Lord
Strange, *5th Earl of*,
24
Derby, William Stanley, *6th
Earl of*, 24
Devereux. *See* Essex
Diana (moon goddess,
Elizabeth I), 111
*Dictionary of National
Biography*, 37, 41, 103,
108
Dido, Queen of Carthage,
107
Drury, *Sir* William, 16
Dudley. *See* Leicester

Earl of Oxford's Men, 26
Earl of Pembroke's Men,
25
Earl of Worcester's Men,
26
Edward II, 107-8
"Edward Bonaventure", 21,
37
Elizabeth I
visit to Hedingham
Castle, 4; in *Hamlet*, 4;
Northern Rebellion
against, 5; at
Westminster
Tournament, 5-6,
arranges E. de Vere's
marriage, 6; and C.
Hatton, 8; and E de
Vere's travels, 8; and

Cathay Company, 12-13; at Audley End, 13; plots against, 5, 16, 17; commits A. Vavasor and E. de Vere to the Tower, 17; payments to E. de Vere, 20-1; and Mary, Queen of Scots, 21; and *Richard II*, 26; death 26-7; as Silvia, 50; and the Duke of Anjou, 98; and H. Wriothesley, 98-100; motto, 98; Gloriana cult, 98-9; and *Edward II*, 108; requires anonymity from E. de Vere, 109; as Belphoebe, Cynthia/Diana, Tellus and Semele, 110-3; as Spenser's Faerie Queene, 98, 123; as Jonson's Queen of Faery, 123-6

Elizabeth Islands, Mass., 83

Endimion (E. de Vere), 110-3, 124-5

Essex, Robert Devereux, *2nd Earl of*, 26

Eumenides (E. de Vere), 111-3

Euphuism, 14-15, 41, 110-3

Faerie Queene, The, 98, 123

Falstaff (Sir John Oldcastle), 42, 124

Faustus. *See Doctor Faustus*

Fenton (in *The Merry Wives of Windsor*), 37-8

Fenton, Edward, 21, 37

Fenton, Geoffrey, 37

Fenton, James, 37-8

First Folio (paid for by Oxford's son-in-law and the son-in-law's brother), 81, 126

Fletcher, John, 116

Florence, 9

Forest of Essex, 27-8

French puns, 54 *passim*

Frobisher, Martin, 12-13

Garnet, Henry, 84

Gaveston, (E. de Vere), 108

Geneva Bible, 19

Genoa, 9

Gertrude (Margaret, *Countess of Oxford*), 4

Gheeraerts, Marcus, *Jr.*, 42

gold, 12-13

Golding, Arthur (E. de Vere's uncle and tutor), 5

Golding, Margaret, *Countess of Oxford*, 3, 4

Golding, Percival, 28

Gosnold, Bartholomew, 83

Gray's Inn, London, 4

Lee, *Sir* Henry, 6
Leicester, Robert Dudley,
   Earl of, 4, 19, 22
Lok, Michael (Shylock),
   12-13, 44
Looney, John Thomas,
   3, 31
Lord Admiral's Men,
   25, 28
Lord Chamberlain's Men,
   24-5
   (then King's Men), 27
Love's Labour's Lost, 16,
   28, 55, 107
Lyly, John, 14-15, 109-18,
   127, 129

Macbeth, 21, 58-60, 84-5
Malvolio (Christopher
   Hatton), 8, 34
Marlowe, Christopher,
   1, 2, 103-9, 114-8,
   121, 127
Marston, John, 118
Mary, Queen of Scots, 5, 16,
   21, 35
Measure for Measure, 11,
   17, 28, 35, 44-5, 55, 57,
   82
Menaphon, 117
Merchant of Venice, The,
   12, 28, 55
Mercutio, 34
Meres, Francis, 25, 108-9
*Merry Wives of Windsor,
   The*, 6, 16, 17, 28, 35,
   37-8, 106, 124-5
Middleton, Thomas, 118

*Midsummer Night's
   Dream, A*, 30-1, 49,
   65-7
Minola, Baptista, 9
Montgomery, Philip
   Herbert, *Earl of*, 25
Montgomery, Susan de
   Vere, *Countess of*, 18
motto, Earl of Oxford's,
   title-page, 33, 39,
   40-80. *See also* puns
Much Ado About Nothing,
   39, 55, 68-70, 72-5

Nashe, Thomas, 117
Netherlands, 19
Nigrone, Baptista, 9
Norfolk, Thomas Howard,
   4th Duke of, 5-7, 12
Norris of Rycote, Francis,
   Lord, 28
Northampton, Lord Henry
   Howard, *afterwards
   Earl of*, 12, 16-17
Northern Rebellion, 5, 85
Northumberland, Earl of, 5
North-West Passage, 12

Ogburn, Charlton, Jr.,
   2-3, 24, 29-32, 37
Ophelia, 6
Othello, 17, 28, 36, 58-60,
   82, 115
Ovid, 5, 29, 123
Oxford, Anne Cecil,
   Countess of (first wife
   of Edward de Vere and

❊   ❊   ❊